I0018505

Artificial Intelligence

A Simplified Guide for Everyone

Nova Martian

© 2024 by **NOBTREX** LLC. All rights reserved.

This publication may not be reproduced, distributed, or
transmitted in any form or by any means, electronic or
mechanical, without written permission from the publisher.
Exceptions may apply for brief excerpts in reviews or
academic critique.

Disclaimer

This book has been created with the assistance of AI tools for content generation, editing, and formatting. While
AI tools have contributed to its development, the content has been reviewed to ensure its quality and accuracy.
Readers are encouraged to approach the material critically and verify information where necessary.

Contents

Introduction

Artificial Intelligence (AI) has firmly established itself as one of the most transformative technologies of the 21st century. As its applications continue to increase at impressive rates, understanding AI is no longer the sole purview of computer scientists or technologists, but a critical subject for the broader society. This book, "Artificial Intelligence: A Simplified Guide for Everyone," aims to demystify AI by offering a clear, accessible, and comprehensive analysis of its key concepts, development, practical applications, and the challenges it presents.

AI refers to the creation of systems that can perform tasks usually requiring human intelligence. These include activities like decision making, language translation, visual perception, and speech recognition, among others. As AI continues to evolve, it exerts a growing influence on nearly every aspect of human life, from healthcare and transportation to communication and entertainment.

The intent of this book is to elucidate the essential components and diverse facets of AI in a way that is accessible yet thorough. Through carefully crafted chapters, readers will explore the historical development of AI, illuminating how foundational theories and technological advancements have shaped its current state. An examination of the core concepts and technologies will provide a critical understanding of the principles and tools that underlie AI systems.

Attention is also directed towards machine learning and deep learning, two pivotal components that continue to drive significant advances in AI capabilities. Understanding these concepts helps highlight why AI is finding increasing applications in fields as varied as medicine, finance, automotive industries, and beyond.

Furthermore, as AI applications become more pervasive, the ethical considerations and societal impacts need closer examination. The book provides thoughtful insights into important discussions about privacy, data security, bias, fairness, and the regulation of AI technologies. We also consider how AI can meet the challenges of the future, proposing scenarios and possibilities that stir the imagination.

By the conclusion of this book, readers will appreciate the complexity, potential, and responsibility that accompany the integration of AI into the fabric of society. This is not merely a survey of technological capabilities but a comprehensive guide that addresses the multifaceted relationship between AI and human progress. In doing so, it stands ready to inform and empower readers to engage with the discourse around AI knowledgeably and constructively.

Chapter 1

Introduction to Artificial Intelligence

Artificial Intelligence is a dynamic and rapidly evolving field focused on creating systems capable of tasks that typically require human intelligence. This chapter offers a foundational perspective on AI, beginning with its definitions and core concepts, and differentiating it from human cognition. It explores the various types of AI, including narrow and general AI, and examines their practical significance in modern life. Furthermore, it addresses the key challenges that arise in AI development, setting the stage for understanding the complexities and capabilities of this transformative technology.

1.1 Understanding Artificial Intelligence

Artificial Intelligence (AI), once the subject of fiction and speculative thought, now plays an increasingly integral role in our daily lives. From suggesting the next song on your playlist to revolutionizing entire industries, AI encompasses a wide array of technologies designed to perform tasks that traditionally require human intelligence. But how did we get here, and what exactly does

AI entail? To truly understand AI, we must begin by unraveling its core concepts, historical milestones, and distinguishing features.

Defining Artificial Intelligence

At its essence, AI is about creating machines or systems that can perform tasks characteristic of human intelligence. These tasks range from problem-solving and pattern recognition to understanding language and making decisions. The goal is not merely to mimic human behavior but to achieve efficiencies or capabilities that exceed those inherent to humans.

The term "Artificial Intelligence" itself was coined in 1956 during a legendary workshop at Dartmouth College. This event is considered a landmark that heralded AI's academic and conceptual identity. The scholars there, including giants like John McCarthy and Marvin Minsky, set forth a vision where machines could simulate every aspect of learning or any other feature of intelligence.

Over the decades, definitions of AI have evolved, reflecting technological advancements and theoretical refinements. Today, AI is broadly categorized into two types: *narrow AI* and *general AI*. Narrow AI is designed for specific tasks, like language translation or playing chess. Most AI applications existing today fall into this category. General AI, a more elusive frontier, aspires to perform any cognitive task at the level of a human being—a goal yet to be realized.

Key Concepts and Components

Understanding AI involves grasping several core concepts and components that form its foundation. Among these, machine learning (ML) is perhaps the most pivotal. ML allows systems to learn from data, identifying patterns, and improving over time without explicit programming. For instance, a recommendation system in an online store utilizes ML to suggest products based on past user behavior.

Another crucial element is *natural language processing* (NLP), which enables machines to understand and respond to human language. NLP facilitates interactions that feel intuitive and human-like, exemplified by virtual assistants like Siri or Alexa that interpret and respond to verbal queries.

AI's capacity to recognize and process images and video is largely thanks to *computer vision*, a field that has seen remarkable advances with technologies such as facial recognition systems. Meanwhile, *robotics* connects AI to the physical world, empowering machines to interpret and act upon sensor data, from autonomous vehicles to industrial robots in manufacturing.

Historical Context and Development

The journey of AI has not been linear, punctuated by periods of hype and funding, followed by frustration and "AI winters" when progress stalled. Its inception took root in the philosophical ponderings of ancient civilizations. The Greeks, for instance, dreamt of automatons capable of assisting humans. However, practical strides only commenced in the 20th century with Alan Turing's proposal of a machine that could compute anything computable— the theoretical groundwork for computers.

The post-war era saw the first digital computers, sparking initial experiments with programs capable of playing chess or solving mathematical theorems. By the late 20th century, neural networks—an attempt to mimic the human brain's architecture—showed promise but also struggled due to computational limits.

The resurgence in AI in the 21st century owed much to several factors: the explosion of data, enhanced processing power, and refined algorithms. Deep learning, a subset of ML involving neural networks with many layers, has achieved breakthroughs in speech and image recognition, reigniting interest and investment in AI.

Applications and Real-World Manifestations

AI's transformative potential is evident across various domains, reshaping how we work, play, and live. In healthcare, AI assists in diagnosing diseases, predicting patient outcomes, and personalizing treatment plans, showing prowess in areas like dermatology where algorithms can outperform human experts.

In finance, AI algorithms evaluate credit risks and detect fraudulent activity with a level of precision and speed unattainable by traditional methods. This automation not only increases accuracy but also reduces costs and operational risks.

Transportation has witnessed a revolution with AI at its helm, from optimizing logistics and supply chains to developing autonomous vehicles. Ride-sharing applications like Uber use AI to match riders optimally, while autonomous cars are programmed to understand and respond to their environment in real-time.

Moreover, in education, AI personalizes learning experiences, adapting to the pace and style of individual students, thereby enhancing engagement and retention. AI's ability to tailor curricula based on data ensures that educational resources reach those who need them most, breaking traditional barriers to learning.

Philosophical and Ethical Considerations

The rise of AI calls into question the nature of intelligence and humanity itself. Philosophers and ethicists debate the implications of creating entities that can think or appear to think. Is an AI's decision grounded in morality, or is it the product of intricate programming lacking genuine understanding?

These considerations extend to ethical concerns around privacy, bias, and autonomy. AI systems can amplify existing biases in data or decision-making, leading to unfair outcomes. Furthermore, as AI takes on more roles traditionally fulfilled by humans, the question of accountability looms large.

Moreover, there are concerns about the impact on employment. While AI can enhance productivity, it might also render certain jobs obsolete, necessitating a societal rethink on work, education, and economic distribution.

The Future of Artificial Intelligence

As AI continues to evolve, its future is both promising and uncertain. Researchers work towards achieving general AI, which, if realized, could redefine the landscape of human and machine collaboration. The prospect of AI possessing emotional intelligence to interact more naturally with humans is on the horizon, opening new avenues in various fields, from mental health care to customer service.

Governments and institutions worldwide are grappling with creating frameworks to manage AI's socio-economic impacts responsibly. The focus is not solely on technological advancement but also on ensuring AI's benefits are equitably distributed and ethically aligned with human values.

Understanding Artificial Intelligence is about more than just the nuts and bolts of technology; it is about recognizing AI's profound implications for society, ethics, and our conception of intelligence itself. As we navigate this rapidly advancing frontier, engaging with these considerations is essential, fostering an informed dialogue that respects both innovation and the intrinsic values at the core of human existence.

1.2   AI vs. Human Intelligence

In the ever-evolving narrative of technological advancement, one intriguing subplot revolves around the comparison between artificial intelligence (AI) and human intelligence. Are machines catching up to our cognitive abilities, or are they simply skilled impostors at best? To unravel this question, we must closely examine the traits that define both AI and human intelligence, exploring how machines measure up against their creators in various aspects.

The Foundation: Computation vs. Cognition

At their core, both AI and human intelligence revolve around problem-solving and understanding the world. However, their approaches differ fundamentally. AI, composed of algorithms and data, processes information through brute-force computation and pattern recognition. It excels in executing vast calculations at an incomprehensible speed and identifying patterns in massive datasets. For instance, AI can analyze gigabytes of customer data to tailor personalized shopping experiences effectively.

Human intelligence, on the other hand, is rooted in cognition—a multifaceted process involving perception, memory, learning, and understanding. It reflects our ability to process emotional and social cues, adapt to new situations, and engage in abstract thought. Unlike AI, whose intelligence is situational and often narrow, human intelligence is flexible and contextually aware.

Historical Perspectives and Developments

The history of AI versus human intelligence is a tale of relentless pursuit. Early AI researchers dreamt of creating machines that could think like humans, their efforts met with enthusiasm and skepticism in equal measure. During the mid-20th century, pioneers like Alan Turing proposed the notion of mechanistic thought, culminating in the Turing Test—a measure of a machine's ability to exhibit intelligent behavior indistinguishable from a human across a range of tasks.

Despite milestones such as IBM's Deep Blue defeating world chess champion Garry Kasparov in 1997, AI's inability to truly mimic human cognition became apparent in what emerged as "AI winters." These were periods characterized by disillusionment and reduced funding due to AI's failure to live up to overhyped expectations.

The 21st century, however, witnessed AI's resurgence, driven by advancements in machine learning and neural networks. Today, AI can translate languages, drive cars, and even outperform doctors in specific diagnostic tests. Yet, this success is bounded by data and computation and remains domain-specific, contrasting with the fluid intelligence displayed by humans.

Capabilities and Limitations

AI systems currently showcase impressive abilities across specific tasks. In terms of data crunching, they leave even the sharpest human minds in the dust. Consider AlphaGo, the AI that defeated a world champion Go player, mastering a game with more potential positions than atoms in the universe. This feat was possible because AI excels at analyzing enormous datasets to identify winning patterns.

Despite these accomplishments, AI's thinking is limited

by its programming and the data it receives. While machines can perform logical reasoning at breakneck speed, they lack the intuitive reasoning and common sense that humans employ when faced with ambiguous scenarios. For instance, AI-driven self-driving cars face challenges with nuanced human gestures and decision-making in unpredictable road conditions—a testament to the machine's lack of deep contextual understanding.

Humans also possess emotional intelligence, enabling us to empathize, connect, and communicate effectively. This social acumen facilitates collaboration, conflict resolution, and creativity—traits machines have yet to master. AI may interpret speech patterns or facial expressions with remarkable accuracy, but it does not "understand" emotions in the human sense.

Interplay Between Intelligences

The interaction between AI and human intelligence opens a panorama of possibilities and challenges. In many fields, humans and AI collaborate effectively, each leveraging the other's strengths. Consider the medical field, where AI assists in diagnosing diseases by analyzing medical images faster and sometimes more accurately than radiologists. Yet, it is the human doctors who contextualize these interpretations within the patient's broader clinical picture.

In creative industries, AI can compose music, suggest edits, or even produce art, but these creations often serve more as starting points for human imagination rather than replacements. An AI-generated jazz tune might lack the soul and spontaneity found in a human performance.

The evolving collaboration between AI and human intelligence is also evident in education, where AI tools personalize learning experiences, yet it is the educators who provide motivation, mentorship, and moral guidance.

Ethical and Philosophical Dimensions

As AI progresses, ethical and philosophical questions regarding the nature of intelligence become paramount. What constitutes true understanding—is it the ability to calculate or the capacity to comprehend emotionally and socially? If an AI system can generate poetic verses or strategic insights, does that equate to creativity or understanding?

Furthermore, the rise of AI poses ethical challenges related to autonomy and accountability. In scenarios where AI decisions impact lives—like self-driving cars determining actions during an accident—questions arise about responsibility and moral agency. Should AI systems be held accountable, or is it the creators or users who should bear this responsibility?

Privacy is another area of concern. AI's reliance on data raises questions about consent and control over personal information. How can we balance AI's potential benefits with the need to protect individual rights?

The Future: Symbiosis or Supremacy?

As we gaze into the future, the debate over AI versus human intelligence evolves from competition to collaboration. While the prospect of creating general AI—machines that can perform any cognitive task on par with humans—remains an ambitious goal, the trajectory suggests a future of symbiosis.

In this envisioned scenario, AI complements human capabilities, alleviating mundane tasks while humans focus on inherently human aspects like empathy, creativity, and critical thinking. This harmonious coexistence embodies the notion that intelligence, whether artificial or human, is not a zero-sum game.

11

Ultimately, the interplay between AI and human intelligence illustrates a dual narrative: one of machines enhancing our ability to tackle complex problems and enhance the human experience, and the other of humans guiding the ethical and purposeful application of technology.

Thus, understanding AI's strengths, recognizing its limitations, and responsibly integrating it into society are key to navigating the future. In this endeavor, remembering the unique value of human intelligence—its capacity for wonder, empathy, and moral discernment—maintains its relevance in a world increasingly shaped by intelligent machines. The quest is not just technological; it is deeply human.

1.3   Types of Artificial Intelligence

Artificial Intelligence (AI) can appear as both a visionary dream and a baffling cornucopia of technological possibilities. As we peel back the layers, we discover that AI isn't a monolithic entity but an intricate assembly of systems and approaches, each with its distinct capabilities and limitations. In this section, we explore the various types of AI, taking a tour through narrow AI, general AI, and beyond, to understand their historical roots, present applications, and future potentials.

Narrow AI: The Master of One

Imagine an octopus in a tuxedo—a curious, efficient specialist in many discrete tasks. This analogy fits Narrow AI, the most prevalent form of AI today. Also known as weak AI, Narrow AI systems are designed to perform singular tasks and do so with superhuman efficiency, yet lack the capacity for general cognition or reasoning beyond their specific functions.

Narrow AI's power is evident in every smartphone's virtual assistant, such as Siri or Google Assistant, which thrives on natural language processing to decipher and respond to requests. In financial services, Narrow AI sorts through mountains of data to detect fraudulent activities faster than any human eye could. When you binge-watch shows on a streaming service, the recommendation algorithm curating your next favorite series is another triumph of Narrow AI, deftly analyzing viewing history to predict preferences.

However, despite these feats, Narrow AI operates within rigid boundaries. This specificity is both its strength and limitation: a chess-playing AI savant stumbles outside its board realm, unable to apply its "intelligence" to draughts, let alone to life's broader challenges. Thus, its intelligence is, by definition, narrow—efficient but confined within predetermined limits.

General AI: The Elusive Ideal

While Narrow AI dazzles with specialization, General AI, or strong AI, embodies an altogether different aspiration: to create machines that possess cognitive abilities equal to that of humans. These systems could theoretically perform any intellectual task a human can, adapting and applying knowledge across a multitude of domains with comprehension and discernment.

The quest for General AI is one of humanity's grand scientific endeavors, stirring both intrigue and speculation. Its concept echoes through popular culture, often depicted in science fiction as robots indistinguishable from humans—not unlike the motifs in "Blade Runner" or the ever-helpful androids of "Star Trek."

Despite the imaginative allure, General AI remains a nascent dream rather than an immediate reality. This pursuit challenges us to not only mimic human cognition in machines but also instill a deep understanding, consciousness, and self-awareness—the nuances of which are not yet fully grasped even in human psychology.

The hurdles are as much philosophical and ethical as they are technological. Can a machine truly possess consciousness, or merely simulate the appearance of it? Should these entities, if realized, be endowed with rights? For now, General AI resides in the realm of frontier research, its horizons extending years, if not decades, into the future.

Superintelligent AI: The Speculative Frontier

Beyond even General AI lies the speculative frontier of Superintelligent AI—a theoretical entity surpassing human intelligence in virtually every aspect, from scientific reasoning to social skills. Unlike General AI, which aims for parity, Superintelligent AI suggests a cognitive leap, opening up profound implications for our role in the universe.

This idea, while captivating, treads delicate ground, challenging us to ponder the consequences of unfettered intelligence. Scholars like Nick Bostrom and tech pioneers such as Elon Musk have voiced both hope and caution, catalyzing discourse around AI as an existential risk and the need for stringent safety measures.

Creating Superintelligent AI is not merely an engineering quest; it's a philosophical odyssey that interrogates the very essence of intelligence, agency, and ethical boundaries. While these discussions are largely speculative, they underscore an urgent need for robust frameworks guiding AI's evolution and integration into society.

Reinforcement Learning: The Playful Prodigy

Among the myriad techniques powering AI, reinforcement learning stands out with its analogy to a curious child learning the ropes of the world. This approach allows AI agents to learn through trial and error, similar to how humans pick up new skills by experimenting with various tactics and receiving feedback based on their successes and failures.

Consider the AI system AlphaGo, which dazzled the world by defeating a professional Go player—a complex game known for its depth and unpredictable plays. This feat was achieved through reinforcement learning, allowing AlphaGo to explore countless board configurations, learn from each outcome, and refine its strategies iteratively.

In practical applications, reinforcement learning extends well beyond games; it has been adeptly integrated into fields like robotics, where autonomous machines learn to navigate their environments, and in optimizing resource allocation in network management.

Transformative Applications Across Sectors

AI's many faces influence diverse sectors, transforming processes and creating new paradigms. In healthcare, AI-powered diagnostics utilize image recognition to identify maladies such as cancers with improved accuracy and speed. In transportation, autonomous vehicles—rooted in complex AI frameworks—promise to revolutionize our concept of personal mobility, enhancing safety and convenience.

The arts haven't been immune to AI's transformative touch, with algorithms generating original music, visual art, and writing. While initially, these creations might appear mechanical, AI-enhanced tools push the boundaries of human creativity, acting as collaborative partners that inspire and augment artistic endeavors.

Moreover, AI optimizes supply chains, predicts consumer trends, and enhances productivity across industries, reducing resource waste while amplifying output. Yet, these advances also pose ethical questions, including those around job displacement and economic disparity, prompting a reevaluation of the socio-economic impacts of AI proliferation.

The Path Forward: Challenges and Opportunities

The proliferation of AI types opens a realm ripe with opportunities and challenges. As AI systems become more sophisticated, questions arise not only about capability but about transparency, ethics, and trust. Ensuring fairness, avoiding bias, and maintaining privacy are paramount as AI is woven into the societal fabric.

Policy and regulation also play crucial roles in shaping AI's future landscape. International frameworks and ethical guidelines are needed to ensure AI is developed and used responsibly, balancing innovation with security and human rights. Collaboration among technologists, ethicists, policymakers, and the public is essential to navigate this intricate terrain, fostering a dialogue that anticipates and addresses AI's multifaceted impact.

Ultimately, AI is more than a collection of algorithms or a futuristic fantasy—it represents an evolving tapestry of human ingenuity and aspiration. Understanding the types of artificial intelligence helps us chart a path that harnesses its potential responsibly, acknowledging that while AI may transform our world, it is humanity's wisdom and values that will guide its journey. As we stand on the brink of unprecedented technological evolution, embracing an informed and proactive stance towards AI's diverse manifestations is crucial to ensuring a future that harmonizes technological advancement with the human spirit.

1.4 Significance of AI Today

In today's world, Artificial Intelligence (AI) is less of a distant vision and more of an ever-present reality, akin to an invisible ether that shapes our daily lives, decisions, and industries. We swiftly move between ideas managed by algorithms, much like threads connecting the vast tapestry of modern society. To understand AI's true significance, we must explore its profound impact across various domains, appreciate the historical context that led us here, and ponder its future trajectory.

The Omnipresence of AI in Daily Life

From the moment we wake up to the buzzing sound of a smartphone alarm, AI's influence begins its gentle intrusion into our routines. Consider the seemingly innocuous journey of how our morning coffee begins with AI-optimized supply chains ensuring beans reach our kitchen before they transform into that essential brew. News apps powered by AI curate articles tailored to our preferences, feeding us information that both informs and isolates based on our reading history.

Let us not forget the perennial digital assistants embedded in our gadgets—Siri, Alexa, Google Assistant—ever-ready to provide directions, answer trivia, or play our favorite tunes. For many, these interactions with AI form a seamless extension of their cognitive and functional capabilities, enhancing productivity and entertainment in equal measure.

AI in Healthcare: Revolutionizing Medicine

17

AI's transformative potential is perhaps most poignantly illustrated in healthcare. As populations age and medical data balloons, AI steps in as both a scalpel and a lifeline, increasing the efficiency and precision of diagnosis and treatment. Machine learning algorithms now scan medical images and identify anomalies with higher accuracy than human radiologists, expediting the detection of conditions like cancer.

Beyond diagnostics, AI plays a pivotal role in drug discovery, shortening development timelines by analyzing chemical compositions and predicting biological interactions. IBM's Watson, initially famed for its game show prowess, now assists in providing personalized treatment recommendations based on a patient's medical history and the latest clinical research.

Telemedicine, accelerated by global events like the COVID-19 pandemic, utilizes AI to triage symptoms and recommend care pathways, reducing the strain on healthcare systems and bringing medical advice to the palm of our hands. However, the integration of AI in healthcare poses ethical concerns regarding privacy, consent, and the need for robust frameworks to protect patient interests.

AI Transforms Industries: Automation and Beyond

Not to be confined to healthcare, AI's industry footprints extend far and wide, revolutionizing sectors ranging from finance to agriculture. In finance, AI algorithms conduct high-frequency trading, optimize investment strategies, and detect fraudulent transactions with unprecedented speed and accuracy, transforming how money flows across the globe.

The agricultural sector, often perceived as immutable, benefits from AI's analytical prowess in predicting weather patterns, monitoring crop health, and optimizing resource use. With the world's population burgeoningly dependent on sustainable food production, AI assists farmers in maximizing yield while minimizing environmental impact.

Manufacturing is another arena where AI's significance cannot be overstated. Factories employ AI-driven robots that assemble products with unmatched precision, conducting quality control processes and predicting maintenance needs before machinery falters. This predict-and-prevent model revolutionizes production efficiency and reduces downtime, cementing AI as an invaluable industrial asset.

AI in Social and Economic Contexts

The societal implications of AI are immense, often heralded as a double-edged sword. On one hand, AI holds the promise of reduced labor demand on mundane tasks, offering individuals more freedom to pursue creative and intellectual activities. On the other, it foments anxiety over job displacement and the polarization of wealth, as automation concentrates value in the hands of those who own and understand the technology.

AI's role in social media platforms is another significant aspect, curating content feeds that, while captivating, may reinforce echo chambers and influence opinions. The algorithm-driven prioritization of content relevant to users' past behaviors raises questions about the nature of choice and autonomy, illustrating the nuanced ramifications of AI's prominence.

Economically, AI can be a catalyst for growth, driving efficiencies that contribute to GDP uplift and national competitiveness. Yet, the challenge lies in equitably deploying these gains across socio-economic strata, ensuring that the benefits of AI do not solely accrue to those already at the technological frontier.

AI and Sustainability: Environmental Impact

In the context of environmental sustainability, AI emerges as both a challenge and a solution. The computational demands of training large AI models consume significant energy, raising concerns about their carbon footprint. However, AI itself offers tools to combat environmental degradation through enhanced monitoring of natural resources, optimizing energy use, and developing innovative solutions in areas like renewable energy forecasting and wildlife conservation.

Advanced AI systems help track deforestation via satellite imagery, alert conservationists to poaching activities, and improve waste management systems through real-time data analysis. By harnessing AI to understand and mitigate ecological challenges, humanity takes strides toward a sustainable coexistence with our planet, though the journey remains long and intricate.

The Ethical Imperative and Regulation

The significance of AI today is inseparable from the ethical dimensions it introduces. AI systems, by their nature, are shaped by the data they process, inherently carrying the potential for bias if trained on unrepresentative or flawed data sets. Organizations must strive to create transparent and accountable AI systems, ensuring they serve rather than detract from democratic values.

Global efforts to regulate AI, such as the EU's discussions on AI ethics and the UN's exploration of AI in sustainable development, highlight the necessity for coherent policies that govern AI's deployment and evolution. These frameworks must balance innovation with precautions to mitigate risks and support equitable societal outcomes.

To foster global cooperation, future dialogues on AI should prioritize inclusivity and representation, ensuring a diverse range of voices contribute to shaping AI's trajectory. The promise of AI as a benevolent force hinges on navigating this moral and ethical labyrinth with clarity, empathy, and wisdom.

AI's Role in Shaping Tomorrow

The significance of AI today is a living narrative, one that is rapidly unfolding and reshaping the contours of human potential and societal function. Its impact on healthcare, industries, social structures, and the environment underlines AI's capacity to redefine the parameters of what is possible, intertwining with our everyday existence in both visible and invisible ways.

As AI continues to progress, the onus is on each of us—researchers, policymakers, technologists, and citizens—to engage with these developments thoughtfully. The future of AI is bright but fraught with challenges; its potential is boundless yet demands careful stewardship. Our collective ability to harness AI responsibly will determine how effectively we transform its significance into a catalyst for inclusive progress and shared prosperity. Whether as a tool, partner, or guide, AI's role in shaping tomorrow calls for an informed and integrated approach, one that preserves the essence of what it means to be human in an increasingly automated world.

1.5 Key Challenges in AI Development

Artificial Intelligence (AI) is often lauded as the marvel of modern technology—a digital philosopher's stone transforming data into unparalleled insights and solutions. Yet, behind this technocratic veneer lie a multitude of challenges that researchers, engineers, and policymakers grapple with as they forge the future of AI. These challenges span the technical, ethical, and social dimensions, each posing questions as intriguing as the answers AI itself seeks to provide. In this section, we explore these multifaceted hurdles, shedding light on the complex reality underpinning AI's development.

Technical Roadblocks: Scaling the AI Model Mountain

At the heart of AI development are the technical challenges that define the boundaries of what these systems can achieve. One principal obstacle is the task of creating algorithms capable of understanding and processing the complexities of the real world more akin to human intelligence. Most AI applications today fall into the category of narrow AI, limited to specific tasks and lacking broader cognitive capabilities—a far cry from the theoretically ambitious general AI.

To address this, AI research focuses on developing more sophisticated machine learning models, particularly those related to deep learning. These models, inspired by the human brain's neural networks, require significant computational resources and vast amounts of data to train effectively. The sheer exponential growth in necessary computational power is a critical impediment to building more advanced and flexible AI systems.

Additionally, ensuring AI models are interpretable and explainable poses another technical barricade. Often called the "black box" problem, many AI systems operate opaquely, producing outcomes without giving clear rationales. This lack of transparency can lead to mistrust or misapplication of AI technologies, especially in sensitive fields like healthcare or finance, where understanding the decision-making process is indispensable.

Data Dilemmas: Sourcing and Sanitizing for Accuracy

Data is the lifeblood of AI, yet obtaining clean, comprehensive, and unbiased data is rife with challenges. AI models' dependency on vast data sets means that ensuring data quality is paramount. Incomplete, inaccurate, or outdated data can skew results, leading to AI systems making erroneous or biased decisions.

Moreover, sourcing data raises significant privacy concerns. Collecting personal data to train AI systems necessitates stringent measures to protect individuals' privacy rights—a complex task given the varying legislations across jurisdictions. There is a pressing need for international cooperation and standardized data protection frameworks to address these concerns adequately.

Bias in AI is another daunting challenge, echoing long-standing societal inequities. AI models can inadvertently perpetuate or even amplify biases present in their training data, leading to discriminatory outcomes. For example, facial recognition systems have shown higher error rates for certain demographic groups, highlighting the critical importance of representative data sets in training AI.

Ethical Conundrums: Navigating the Moral Maze

As AI's capabilities expand, so do the ethical questions surrounding its development and use. These dilemmas extend beyond technical considerations, touching upon fundamental issues of fairness, accountability, and transparency. One major ethical challenge is ensuring AI systems are deployed in ways that benefit the broader spectrum of society, rather than concentrating power in the hands of a few.

There is also the ethical quandary of AI-driven decisions impacting human lives in areas like criminal justice, hiring, and financial lending. These systems need to be fair and free from discrimination—no small feat given that the algorithms reflect the biases in their training data.   Ensuring fairness requires deliberate design choices, continuous monitoring, and recalibration of AI systems to mitigate these biases.

Furthermore, AI systems' potential to manipulate information or influence public discourse raises additional ethical concerns.   Governments and organizations must work to prevent AI from being used maliciously to spread misinformation or engage in surveillance without consent, maintaining ethical standards that safeguard public trust.

Regulatory Hurdles: Crafting Suitable Policies

AI development occurs in a rapidly changing landscape where regulation often struggles to keep pace with technological advances. Crafting effective policies that balance innovation with societal safeguards is no trivial task. There is a delicate balance between fostering an environment conducive to AI research and ensuring AI applications are safe, reliable, and ethical.

Regulatory frameworks must adapt quickly to consider issues like liability when AI systems falter, intellectual property rights as AI creates or innovates, and data protection standards across different regions. International collaboration is crucial, given AI's inherently global impact.

European Union regulations like the General Data Protection Regulation (GDPR) and upcoming AI-specific legislation illustrate attempts to address such challenges, mandating transparency and accountability. Meanwhile, other nations explore their regulatory regimes, leading to a patchwork of guidelines that may complicate global compliance for AI developers.

Economic and Social Impacts: Addressing the Human Aspect

Amid discussions of AI's technical and regulatory challenges, one must not overlook its economic and social repercussions. As AI systems automate more tasks, the workforce faces challenges adapting to an ever-evolving job market. While AI has the potential to create new job sectors and augment human performance, it also threatens to displace workers in specific industries—raising questions about the future of work and equitable economic transition.

Dialogue surrounding universal basic income, continuous education, and workforce retraining initiatives gains traction as societies confront the disruptions driven by AI. Ensuring that AI's benefits are shared equitably across socio-economic classes remains a pivotal challenge for policymakers.

The interplay between AI and social structures further extends to issues of digital accessibility and inequality. Bridging the digital divide is crucial to ensuring that AI advancements do not exacerbate existing disparities but rather contribute to a more inclusive society.

Future Prospects: A Collaborative Effort

Navigating the key challenges in AI development is a collective endeavor, requiring collaboration across multiple disciplines and sectors. As AI continues to evolve, prioritizing interdisciplinary research and incorporating diverse perspectives will be essential to address the multifaceted hurdles effectively.

Stakeholders from academia, industry, public sectors, and civil society must engage in open dialogues, crafting holistic strategies that integrate technical innovation with ethical, legal, and social considerations. Investing in AI education and literacy is vital to empower individuals to understand and engage with AI systems critically, fostering an informed and proactive populace ready to leverage AI's potential responsibly.

Moreover, the quest for explainable and accountable AI grows in importance, pushing developers to reformulate models that prioritize transparency, user understanding, and trustworthiness.

Charting a Balanced Path Forward

The challenges in AI development are as varied as they are complex, reflecting the broader narrative of AI as both a technological breakthrough and a societal paradigm shift. Addressing these challenges requires an agile, interdisciplinary approach that embraces technical prowess, ethical foresight, thoughtful regulation, and proactive public policy.

AI's path forward must be one that is cognizant of its impact, striving to harness its promise while mitigating potential pitfalls. Through collaborative effort and thoughtful stewardship, the future of AI can be shaped as a tool for collective advancement, guided by principles that reflect the best of human values and societal aspirations. As we embrace AI's transformative potential, ensuring it serves humanity as a mutual ally rather than an unbridled disruptor will be key to unlocking its true significance for generations to come.

Chapter 2

Historical Development of AI

The historical development of Artificial Intelligence traces its roots from mid-20th century theoretical perspectives to its establishment as a distinct field of study. This chapter examines the pivotal eras in AI's evolution, including its inception during the 1950s and 1960s, the challenges of AI winters, and subsequent revivals that were marked by technological breakthroughs. By exploring key contributions and innovations, it provides a comprehensive overview of how past advancements have shaped the present landscape of AI research and application, highlighting the milestones that continue to influence the field today.

2.1 The Origins of AI

To understand Artificial Intelligence (AI), one might imagine a scene from a science fiction film where machines outsmart humans. But the origins of AI are not rooted in such cinematic dramatizations. Instead, they spring from a fertile blend of philosophy, logic, mathematics, cybernetics, and early computer science – fields that ponder the nature of human thought and the potential for machines to emulate it.

The intellectual seeds of AI were sown in ancient times, where philosophers from diverse cultures asked foundational questions about human cognition. Questions like "Can machines think?" echo the musings of early thinkers who debated whether human thought could be replicated by a non-human entity. One might point to Descartes' famous assertion, "Cogito, ergo sum" (I think, therefore I am), as an early exploration of the relationship between the mind and the possibility of artificial entities possessing a cognitive dimension.

Moving forward in history, the Enlightenment brought rational inquiry to the forefront. The notion of mechanistic reasoning, popular among philosophers such as Leibniz and Hobbes, posited that logical reasoning could be formalized much like arithmetic. Imagine a 'logical calculus' that could, in theory, process any thought or problem. Although the circuits and algorithms of today's AI were not yet conceptualized, these ideas laid down the bedrock for later developments.

The formal roots of what we recognize today as AI emerged in the 20th century, against a backdrop of rapid technological and theoretical advancements. Here is where the magic truly begins: the mid-century confluence of computer science and cognitive science. Inspired by Alan Turing's seminal 1950 paper, "Computing Machinery and Intelligence," the field began to take a more concrete shape. Turing proposed the now-famous test that bears his name—a measure of a machine's ability to exhibit intelligent behavior indistinguishable from that of a human. Imagine the thrill of this time when the notion of a thinking machine stepped out of the pages of fantastical science fiction and began to nudge its way into academic discourse.

It was Turing's vision of a "universal machine" that could, given appropriate instructions, harness the potential to solve any computable problem, which provided a pivotal spark for AI's genesis. The implications were profound—a machine capable of processing logical arguments and learning from experiences, simulating intelligence. Yet, practical realizations of these theories were hindered by the limitations of early computers.

Turning attention to the 1940s and 1950s, we uncover the simultaneous emergence of cybernetics. By envisioning and developing systems of control and communication in organisms and machines, pioneers like Norbert Wiener explored processes that resemble today's AI, such as feedback loops and learning from the environment. Cybernetic principles hinted at the possibility of machines that could adapt and potentially emulate human cognitive functions—a key tenet of AI research.

In the foundational year of 1956, the Dartmouth Conference was convened. Within the confines of this historic gathering, the term "Artificial Intelligence" was coined, marking the official birth of AI as a research field. John McCarthy, Marvin Minsky, Nathaniel Rochester, and Claude Shannon, among others, envisaged an ambitious goal: to make machines use language, form abstractions, and solve problems hitherto confined to the realm of human thought. Despite technological and theoretical limitations, this meeting catalyzed a newfound partnership between cognitive science and computer engineering, birthing a community dedicated to the exploration of intelligent machines.

Early AI programs seemed imbued with an almost magical capability. Programs developed in subsequent years demonstrated prowess in specific tasks, like playing chess or proving mathematical theorems. Newell and Simon's Logical Theorist, which mimicked human problem-solving processes, and subsequent passage of Goldberg's machine learning experiments were pivotal milestones.   These developments, while limited by modern standards, demonstrated substantial headway in automated logical reasoning and laid the groundwork for further advances.

However, breathless optimism soon waned when AI researchers faced real-world complexities far surpassing the neatly defined problems their algorithms initially tackled. Despite promising developments, the obstacles of limited computing power and the technological realities of the time led to a sluggish tempering of expectations.

Throughout the fledgling years of AI, discussions about symbolic versus connectionist approaches simmered within academic circles.   Symbolic AI, aligned with the early logical reasoning pioneers, posited that human intelligence could be represented through the manipulation of symbols and rules. Conversely, connectionist approaches, still in their infancy, suggested that intelligence emerges from the interplay of simpler processing units, echoing neural networks within the human brain.   This early debate continued to influence AI's evolutionary trajectory, underpinning both setbacks and breakthroughs encountered in subsequent decades.

Beyond the academic realm, one might muse on how these foundational years shaped public perception of AI. We see a pattern of enthusiasm embroiled with skepticism—a narrative oscillating between the dream of intelligent machines and the pragmatic challenges of constructing them.   This cultural oscillation, rooted in these origins, persists even as modern AI systems demonstrate capacities that could only be dreamt of by those early visionaries.

Thus, the origins of AI provide a rich tapestry where speculative philosophy meets ambitious scientific inquiry. In contemplating how far AI has come since Turing's musings and the first forays at Dartmouth, one cannot help but marvel at the journey. The path from theoretical musings to tangible machine capabilities is one of steady innovation, profound discoveries, and the relentless pursuit of the question: Can machines think? As we shall see in subsequent sections, AI's historical path is peppered with periods of both dormancy and explosive growth—each formative and informing the remarkable leaps made in recent years, yet deeply anchored in the inquisitive spirit of its origins.

The story of AI's origins is not just a chronicle of technological advancements but a testament to humanity's enduring quest to understand and replicate its cognitive essence. It is a narrative of pioneers daring to dream of a world where machines mirror, if not surpass, the intellectual domains once thought the exclusive preserve of human intelligence. It is into this continuing journey that we delve as we explore the dawn, nadirs, and breakthroughs of AI's storied evolution.

2.2   The Dawn of AI Research

The dawn of AI research marks a thrilling chapter in the history of both science and technology. It was a time when intrepid minds came together to explore the prospect of machines capable of exhibiting human-like intelligence. While today's world is increasingly populated with AI-powered applications, the path to this future was paved in the 1950s and 1960s by pioneers who conducted pioneering research and embarked on groundbreaking projects.

Imagine a whirl of excitement at the 1956 Dartmouth Conference, the seminal event where researchers first congregated to define and explore Artificial Intelligence as a formal discipline.   This conference, convened by luminaries like John McCarthy, Marvin Minsky, Nathaniel Rochester, and Claude Shannon, was not merely an episodic gathering. It was a catalyst, seeding a global community committed to unravelling the mysteries of artificial cognition.

At Dartmouth, a collective and electrifying vision emerged: machines that could learn, self-correct, and understand human instructions.   AI was not yet anchored in science fiction robots or omnipresent digital assistants, but in a quest to forge autonomous systems that could conduct tasks requiring human-like reasoning and adaptability.

In this golden epoch of AI's nascent years, researchers undertook ambitious projects that would set the stage for decades of innovation. A particularly iconic project was Newell and Simon's development of the Logic Theorist. Imagine a machine designed to mimic human reasoning as it tackled the intricacies of high school geometry proofs. Upon its debut, the Logic Theorist successfully proved 38 of the 52 theorems from Whitehead and Russell's *Principia Mathematica*, even stumbling upon a new, simpler proof than those documented by its human predecessors. This work laid the foundational principles of symbolic AI and demonstrated that automated reasoning could parallel human problem-solving processes.

Another landmark development of the era was the General Problem Solver (GPS), also conceived by Newell and Simon. This machine made further strides in demonstrating the potential of symbolic manipulation. The GPS was a trailblazer in creating computer systems that attempted to emulate human problem-solving strategies across a range of domains—from chess to mathematical logic. Observers were captivated by its application of means-ends analysis, a strategy to reduce discrepancies between current states and desired outcomes. Although the dreams of a fully versatile GPS were hubristic in hindsight, the project expanded our understanding of the complexities inherent in abstract reasoning—a contribution of enduring significance.

As the 1960s unfolded, funding, interest, and excitement around AI swelled, buoyed by soaring expectations of what machines might achieve. Federally funded programs such as the Massachusetts Institute of Technology's (MIT) AI Laboratory and the Stanford Research Institute positioned the United States as a global leader in this burgeoning field. Meanwhile, the renowned British mathematician and logician Alan Turing continued to fuel imaginations as his eponymous test navigated its way into popular consciousness, challenging the world to ponder machines' potential for replicating human-like intelligence.

Symbolic AI was not the only paradigm competing for prominence during AI's formative years. Parallel endeavors in the domain of connectionism unfolded, exploring how artificial neural networks might mirror biological processes. Frank Rosenblatt's Perceptron, developed in 1958, represents one of the earliest attempts to harness computing machinery inspired by neural constructs found in the human brain. This early neural network hinted at the ability to recognize patterns and categorize inputs dynamically—prospective capabilities pivotal to many of today's AI applications.

Projects like Rosenblatt's Perceptron championed an alternative to symbolic reasoning. However, the narrative of the late 50s and 60s came with its fair share of drama—beautiful triumphs tempered by stinging criticisms. Scholars like Marvin Minsky cast skepticism on neural networks, pointing out inherent limitations, such as difficulties in solving non-linearly separable problems.   His critique contributed to a decline in neural network research—a precursor to what we now recognize as an AI winter.

But before any cold spells took hold, the tantalizing hopes and early successes promoted a sensational wave of optimism.   AI researchers embarked upon a suite of initiatives that seemed to promise a world where machines could conduct tasks from insights to speech recognition.   Notable endeavors included Shakey the Robot, a project developed at the Stanford Research Institute, which demonstrated the potential integration of robotic systems with AI to perform complex tasks, albeit in structured environments.

Shakey's autonomous navigation and decision-making served as a predecessor to today's autonomous vehicles. Equipped with sensors and algorithms to perceive— imagine this—a defined warehouse-like world, Shakey established a celebrated precedent for real-time AI and robotics integration.

The optimistic horizons of AI during its early research stages envisioned machines augmenting and outmaneuvering human capacities.   Researchers sought applications encompassing language translation, medical diagnoses, and even military simulations. As we explore these early ambitions, however, one observes a pattern that would come to define much of AI's development: an oscillation between aspiration and the stark realities of technological and theoretical constraints.

By the late 1960s, researchers grappled with frustrating complexities that eluded their initially simplified models. The limitations of computing power and algorithms, compounded by the lack of comprehensive databases, served as repeated reminders that AI research required not only ingenuity but patience and significant investment. These challenges foreshadowed the difficulty of implementing real-world AI systems that matched researchers' visions.

'Twas not all battles without spoils. Important theoretical frameworks emerged during this time, such as John McCarthy's invention of the Lisp programming language—an artifact still essential to many AI applications today. Lisp became the lingua franca of AI programming, revered for its flexibility in symbolic expression and its fit within recursive logic processing—hallmarks of early AI development.

However, the same unrestricted optimism that propelled an age of boundless curiosity gave rise to bold promises that repeatedly found themselves at odds with what was technically feasible. The lure of intelligent machines operating seamlessly in human environments proved more complex than could have been imagined by those pioneer researchers, who gambled on AI's potential to both define and redefine the contours of modern existence.

In this heady landscape of promise and pragmatism, pathbreaking advancements and these varied efforts coalesced into a profound investigation into what machine-generated intellect might look like. The roll of dice taken by these early AI architects paved the edifice upon which modern advances rise.

As we transition through the storied decades of AI, one should indeed remember that the dawn of AI research was a mosaic—an ambitious yet logical step into the unknown, an era glowing with intellectual exploration and the anticipation of what machines, when mounted with the right instructions and data, could achieve. It is this junction between unbounded curiosity and rigorous study that has brought humanity closer to realizing hearts and minds in silicon—a pursuit continued apace by the AI community through both winter and thaw.

2.3   AI Winters and Revivals

The story of Artificial Intelligence is not merely a tale of relentless progress but rather one resembling the changing seasons—a series of alternating winters and vibrant awakenings. This alternating cycle of ebbs and flows marked AI's journey, punctuated by moments of great hope and periods of profound disillusionment.

These AI winters represent episodes marked by waning interest, reduced funding, and skepticism about the potential of AI technology. Yet, paradoxically, it was in the wake of each winter that AI experienced revivals—times of renewed vigor fueled by breakthroughs in computational power, theoretical advancements, and emerging applications.

To truly appreciate AI winters, one must understand the backdrop against which they occurred. The earliest AI research, burgeoning with untamed optimism, set expectations stratospherically high. It was hubris, but also an era sparked by machine triumphs over narrowly defined tasks. Yet the reality was gravitational: AI research hit its first major obstacles when the tangible application of these accomplishments lagged behind the promises being made.

One could argue that the glorious summer preceding the first AI winter heated the ground beyond its ability to bear fruit. This first winter arrived in the 1970s, a decade shadowed by the limitations in hardware, especially given the ambitious aims set forth by early enthusiasts. Computers of that epoch simply lacked the processing power needed to deliver on AI's grandiose visions.

During the 1960s, expectations soared with projects demonstrating early AI's promise in logical reasoning and problem-solving. However, the complexity of programming and computing deficiencies delivered a sobering blow. Rendered ineffective by slow-processing systems and insufficient memory, initial AI systems struggled with basic tasks beyond constrained environments. The critics pounced, characterizing these impediments as emblematic of AI's fundamental flaws, labeling its ambitions as little more than a "grandiose speculation."

Further amplifying the winter chill was the Lighthill Report of 1973. Commissioned by the British government, this report was intended to evaluate the progress of AI research in the United Kingdom. Its conclusions were stark, outlining AI's far-reaching failures to meet its goals. The result was a dramatic curtailment of funding, leaving AI research in Britain virtually dormant.

While Europe experienced its chill, a similar freeze was unfolding across the Atlantic. In the United States, DARPA (Defense Advanced Research Projects Agency), a significant sponsor of AI research, grew impatient with the absence of tangible returns on their investment. Funding was rerouted to projects promising quicker, more tangible outcomes.

Yet as with nature, no winter lasts indefinitely. Enter the revival—a phoenix-like resurgence emerging in the early 1980s. A particularly intriguing development was the introduction and popularization of expert systems.

Designed to simulate the decision-making ability of a human expert, these systems offered a promising pathway
outside traditional, labor-intensive symbolic AI models.

An exemplar of this revival was the development of
systems like XCON at Digital Equipment Corporation,
which optimized configurations of computer orders.
These systems were not only scientifically fascinating
but also offered genuine economic value, rekindling
interest and investment in AI pursuits.   With this
tangible utility of AI initiatives validated, funding
flowed back into academia, with governments and
corporates eager for the competitive edge these systems
might offer.

The mid-1980s heralded yet another pivotal moment for
AI, marked by an upsurge in connectionist approaches—
an area temporarily forsaken in earlier decades.   In
particular, the resurgence of neural networks provided
new avenues for exploration.   Unlike traditional
symbolic AI, this approach explored the emulation
of the human brain's networks, preferring pattern
recognition over logic-based methods.   Bolstered by
the improved computational power of the era, neural
networks gained momentum, shedding a newfound
perspective on learning models.

Intriguing the world over, these networks displayed capacities like image and speech recognition, challenging
the boundaries of what machines could achieve in mimicking human faculties. With the horn of opportunity
in hand, the revival pushed AI research to rethink its
foundational postulates and direction.

Despite these newfound prospects of the 1980s, an in-
convenient truth for AI loomed: the winters had taught
that triumph required tempered expectations, realigned
goals, and clarity of implementation. Both the ebullient

outcomes of neural approaches and humbling lessons of prior disappointments necessitated a balanced plan of action, aiming to avoid another cycle of disillusionment.

AI's second winter followed as the 1990s approached. A surge of interest peaked before receding into skepticism once more—a retreat attributed to the failure of expert systems to fully deliver on their expansive potential. The complexity and costliness of maintaining such systems led to apparent futility in reproducing human-like thought processes. Unchecked, the industry began to scale down investment, refocusing efforts on other technological frontiers deemed more promising.

There are echoes in the present of these cyclical challenges, illustrating that revivals have emerged when AI research reframes and redirects efforts toward realistic and incremental objectives. The early 2000s, however, heralded an awakening of significance. This new chapter emerged, fueled by fundamental shifts in data availability and computational advancements. As storage became affordable, and as the internet burgeoned, a data deluge swept across the AI landscape. Machine learning, an AI subfield that leveraged vast data pools to unravel intricate patterns, stepped into the limelight.

A crucial revitalization came with breakthroughs in algorithms, notably deep learning and its architecture, convolutional neural networks (CNNs). These frameworks proved integral to revolutionary progress in fields like image recognition, natural language processing, and autonomous systems. By feeding on vast oceans of data, these models demonstrated unprecedented accuracy in deciphering images, producing text, and offering recommendations—usable results that declared AI's potency more convincingly than grand narratives ever could.

This new AI spring, unique in its blend of technological, theoretical, and practical feasibility, was reinforced by burgeoning interest from tech giants like Google, Amazon, and Facebook. Encouraged by the technological promise, the corporate sector began to invest heavily in AI research and developments, integrating learnings into everyday applications. AI was no longer a pursuit confined to academia; it became a cornerstone of innovation strategies worldwide.

As a reflection on these seasons of AI, one recognizes that winters are not merely periods of inactivity and futility. They serve as vital resets—contemplative moments of recalibration. It is during these intervals that AI architects reconsider goals, strategize anew, and envisage technologies beyond contemporary constraints.

In the present epoch of AI revival, the lessons of history underscore the importance of advancement tempered by realism, application grounded in utility, and the necessity for continuous dialogues between developers and societal stewards. The enduring rhythms of AI's past teach that winters are an integral precursor to eventual spring—the dawn following dusk—within this perpetually evolving journey AI navigates.

Thus unfolds the narrative of AI's cyclical fortune—a tapestry of setbacks and triumphs, skepticism and innovation. It is through these dynamic seasons that AI matured, shaping the technologies that have ushered AI from era-defining winters to the transformative resurgence we witness today.

2.4 Breakthroughs in AI Technology

In the captivating odyssey of Artificial Intelligence (AI), specific technological breakthroughs serve as pivotal milestones, guiding the field from hopeful conjecture to practical marvel. These breakthroughs not only illuminated AI's potential but also reshaped industries and everyday life. As we navigate through these moments of innovation, we uncover how they laid the foundation for modern AI applications, marking progress across tasks once dominated by human ingenuity.

Imagine the world in the late 20th century, where dreams of intelligent machines were encumbered by hardware limitations and theoretical conundrums. It was the era where AI, fresh from its wintery setbacks, embarked on journeys to resolve its perennial challenges. Breakthroughs in computational power, algorithmic design, and data availability set AI on a transformative course—a tour de force that would redefine what machines could achieve.

One of the seminal developments that marked a turning point for AI was the resurgence of interest in neural networks during the 1980s. Although initially conceived in the 1940s, neural networks languished during early AI winters due to limited computing capabilities. Fast forward to the 1980s, when key advances like the backpropagation algorithm reenergized this approach. Often likened to teaching machines through example, backpropagation enabled multi-layer perceptrons to learn complex representations, propelling them into the spotlight. The true genius of this breakthrough was its capacity to refine the network's weights iteratively, reducing errors and improving predictive accuracy. This method proved indispensable in tasks that went beyond simple logical operations to the more nuanced realms of vision and speech.

Fast-forward to the modern era, when this renewed interest set the stage for another quantum leap: deep learning. Advances in computational power, coupled with vast, readily available datasets, facilitated the development of deep learning architectures like convolutional neural networks (CNNs) and recurrent neural networks (RNNs). These architectures provided machines with layered hierarchical models capable of extracting intricate features and temporal patterns from raw data. This represented a radical departure from the brittle symbolic approaches that dominated early AI research.

Deep learning's first major triumph came in 2012 with AlexNet, a notable entry in the ImageNet Large Scale Visual Recognition Challenge. This deep convolutional neural network achieved a top-five error rate of 15.3%, drastically outperforming the second runner-up. A moment of AI history made tangible through pixels, AlexNet legitimized deep learning's potential, catalyzing a chain-reaction of adoption and adaptation across computer vision tasks. It was a watershed for AI—a demonstration that machines could not only perceive but also distinguish between millions of dimensions with uncanny accuracy.

The advent of deep learning did not limit itself to visual acuity alone. Natural language processing (NLP), a field where machines seek to comprehend human language, also witnessed transformative breakthroughs. Early on, AI researchers grappled with the exhaustive rule-based systems typical of generative linguistics. Meanwhile, statistical methods sought to parse language structures through probabilities and patterns. Enter word embeddings and neural network-based language models, which elevated the meaning distillation process by mapping words into continuous vector spaces. Models like Word2Vec and subsequent advancements like TensorFlow's BERT—Bidirectional Encoder Representations from Transformers—demonstrated unprecedented capabilities in capturing context, semantics, and nuances of natural language.

Deep learning's proficiency across vision and language heralded a new chapter of AI sophistication—machines capable of performing feats that ranged from object detection and automatic translation to understanding sentiment and generating creative textual content. As machine abilities mushroomed, so did applications in areas as diverse as autonomous vehicles, healthcare diagnostics, recommendation systems, and beyond.

An often unsung yet transformative contribution was the emergence of generative adversarial networks (GANs), introduced by Ian Goodfellow and his team in 2014. This groundbreaking architecture, a masterwork of creative antagonism, pitched two networks—one generative and one discriminative—against each other. By training each to outwit the other, GANs generated outputs that closely mimicked real data. From photorealistic images and video synthesis to drug discovery and fashion design, GANs made it plausible to create, not just compute, meshing creativity with computation.

Robotics, too, found itself revolutionized through AI advancements. Thanks to AI's breakthroughs, robots transitioned from the realm of industrial assembly lines into environments demanding more delicate human interactions. With machine learning algorithms expanding their capacity to learn from dynamic environments and past data, robots found roles in healthcare as surgical assistants, in households as personalized aides, and in exploration missions as resilient navigators. Illustrative of this transformation is Boston Dynamics' Atlas—a humanoid robot capable of negotiating obstacles with dexterity reminiscent of human agility, an exhibition of intelligent engineering in motion.

The domain of autonomous systems, perhaps one of AI's most polychromatic manifestations, has further spotlighted the significance of AI technology breakthroughs. At the heart of autonomous vehicles are sophisticated AI systems capable of processing sensor inputs, making split-second decisions, and continuously learning from environmental contexts. Self-driving cars, from Tesla to Waymo, epitomize how far AI's footprints have traversed—not merely on urban streets but into broader societal dialogues surrounding ethics, regulation, and the future of transportation.

AI's thoughtful meddlings found resonance in health-care, a realm where its influence is as spectacular as it is life-changing. Machine learning algorithms ventured into predictive analytics, where tasks like diagnosing diseases from radiological images or tailoring personalized treatment plans became not only feasible but transformational. AI solutions such as IBM Watson Health, which analyzes medical literature and patient records to suggest treatment options, showcase AI's practical potential to augment human expertise in pinpointing precise medical interventions.

Yet, even as AI matures, its breakthroughs provoke questions probing ethics and implementation. It opens doors to philosophical debates: Can AI be harnessed without biases that reflect and amplify societal inequalities?   How does one safeguard privacy in an interconnected world brimming with data-intensive applications?   These are the crucial dialogues that contemporize AI's journey, ensuring that technological strides align harmoniously with human-centric values.

In considering the labyrinthine course of AI's breakthroughs, one cannot ignore the significance of democratization. The open-source ethos, embraced by community-led platforms like TensorFlow and

PyTorch, has dismantled barriers to AI development, accelerating innovation and introducing AI education to bright minds across geographies. The synergy between academia, industry, and open-source initiatives marks this juncture as an epoch where collective genius catalyzes shared progress.

Thus, from virtual perception and speech imitation to dexterous mechanical automation, breakthroughs in AI technology have reshaped conversations across intellectual and industrial domains, kindling endless possibilities. These pioneering milestones have transformed an aspirational theory into the bedrock of modern technological infrastructure—reminding us that AI's saga, interwoven with societal realities, offers a continuous promenade from the conceivable to the unfathomable.

Endearingly multifaceted and dynamically evolving, the breakthroughs of AI technology, past and present, en-capsulate a breathtaking expedition—a lively dance between dreams, cognition, and hardware. They are emblematic of a dialogue between humanity's deepest curiosities and the ever-expanding horizons of intelligence, design, and utility. Here's to speculating where the next breakthrough might arise, ever-aware that within AI's transformative nucleus dwells a promise: to understand human essence in the syntax of zeros and ones.

2.5 Recent Advances and Trends

In traversing the cutting-edge of Artificial Intelligence (AI), we're beckoned into a landscape defined by rapid innovation and transformative potential. Recent advances in AI technology have transcended mere academic curiosity, driving unprecedented shifts across industries and societies. As we journey through these developments, we encounter a mélange of ingenuity and practical applications that are reshaping the way we interact with the world—ushering in an era where boundaries between human cognition and machine capabilities are increasingly blurred.

One of the remarkable strides in AI is the continued evolution of machine learning, particularly deep learning architectures. Driven by the potent combination of vast datasets, enhanced computational power, and sophisticated algorithms, deep learning has become the cornerstone of AI advancements. Contemporary developments in this area have led to the creation of expansive models like GPT-3, which boast billions of parameters, enabling machines not only to respond but engender meaningful conversations, generate texts, and even write coherent essays—much like the one you are currently reading.

The scale and ambition of models such as GPT-3 signal a breakthrough in natural language processing (NLP)—endowing machines with an understanding of language that is nuanced, contextually aware, and surprisingly human-like. This extends far beyond simple grammar parsing to the comprehension of subtleties, idioms, and cultural nuances—a feat once thought insurmountable in the realm of artificial cognition.

AI's linguistic prowess finds applications in areas as varied as customer service bots that provide seamless interactions, to tools aiding writers in crafting narratives. Picture crafting a story where your AI companion suggests metaphors, adjusts tones, and corrects linguistic faux pas with a familiar expertise akin to a seasoned editor. Within legal settings, AI software now reviews contracts, identifying discrepancies faster than human solicitude. Medicine hasn't been left untouched; AI accelerates drug discovery with solutions that parse existing literature for compound relationships and predict molecular behavior with uncanny precision.

Another burgeoning trend is the movement towards AI democratization. In an age characterized by technological accessibility, developers and organizations worldwide are increasingly prioritizing open platforms and collaborative ecosystems. The ethos of open innovation underscores the last decade, manifested through community-led efforts like OpenAI, TensorFlow, and PyTorch. These initiatives have made sophisticated AI tools accessible to amateurs and professionals alike—fueling creativity and decentralizing innovation.

Industries that once viewed AI as a distant frontier now see it as integral to competitiveness and strategy. Take, for instance, the financial sector, which harnesses AI for algorithmic trading, credit scoring, and fraud detection. AI algorithms tirelessly sift through terabytes of transaction data to detect patterns invisible to the ordinary statisticians' eye, allowing for real-time risk assessment and decision-making unparalleled in speed and accuracy.

The marvels of AI are vividly illustrated in autonomous systems, perhaps best exemplified by self-driving vehicles. The dream of autonomous transportation silently transitioning from sci-fi reverie to tangible reality is reshaping urban planning, logistics, and the very ethos of human mobility. Companies like Tesla and Waymo are pioneering these advances by employing AI technologies that crunch streams of sensory data into navigational decisions. These intelligent systems seamlessly balance speed, traffic conditions, pedestrian movement, and road obstacles—efforts underwritten by machine learning models designed to learn from each drive's vast palette of information.

Yet, as AI permeates our lives, it sparks multifaceted discussions about ethics and governance. Recognizing the social implications of AI technologies, scholars and practitioners are rallying around the responsible AI movement—prioritizing transparency, fairness, and accountability in deploying intelligent systems. These concerns are at the vanguard of AI design, prompting regulators to draft legislation and ethical guidelines that enshrine privacy and mitigate biases.

The interplay of AI with ethics has notably emphasized the need for explainability. Amidst burgeoning calls for accountability, the black-box nature of many AI models has come under scrutiny. In remedying this, techniques such as model interpretability and explainable AI (XAI) are gaining traction—ensuring stakeholders comprehend AI's decision processes and trust their outcomes. Such endeavors are crucial, for in a world where machines make consequential decisions, the insights we glean from them need to be as clear as their accuracy asserts.

In exploring the current AI zeitgeist, the symbiotic relationship between humans and machines takes center stage—transformative automation intertwined with human-oriented design. The rise of human-centric AI celebrates augmenting rather than replacing human capabilities, fostering collaboration and creating value across domains. Artists employ AI to generate music that pushes creative boundaries, engineers leverage machine intelligence to optimize complex workflows, and educators use AI tutors to personalize instruction— each demonstrating AI's ubiquity in enhancing lived experiences.

Sustainability and AI together plot another significant

trend. As global focus sharpens on climate change, AI applications in environmental monitoring and resource management have taken the evolutionary leap. Machine learning models predict weather patterns, optimize energy usage in smart grids, and model ecological impacts—serving as the analytical bedrock for meeting ambitious global sustainability goals. Companies are adopting AI-powered solutions to monitor and optimize supply chains, ensuring pathways that reduce carbon footprints while maintaining efficiency.

The era of AI singularity, where its autonomy and intelligence rival human faculties, might yet remain an elusive prospect. However, it is undeniable that the AI field is more vibrant and impactful than ever—a movement that transcends generation and geography, oscillating on the principle of enhancing potentialities and nudging humanity toward unforeseen prospects.

Glancing toward the horizon, one sees yet another dynamic line: the integration of AI with quantum computing—thought to unravel computational problems exponentially faster, positing prospects that could dwarf contemporary AI feats. The emergence of AI-augmented quantum algorithms points to a future wherein computations enabling real-world AI applications become drastically efficient and powerful, opening up further avenues of exploration.

Embedding ourselves within this zeitgeist of progress, curiosity, and reflection, we acknowledge both the transformations AI ushers in and the dialogues it necessitates. The synthesis of human ingenuity and algorithmic proficiency underscores the 21st century's AI journey—an epoch defined by exploration and dialogue. It invites us into incessant questioning while forever casting an eye on the evolving narrative, captivating in its mysteries and radiant with potential.

Crafted in this confluence, the recent advances and trends in AI cast a bright luminescence that playfully teases our imagination, suggesting a future interwoven with possibilities that exceed even our grandest aspirations. It is this delicate dance of innovation and introspection that will define how AI's journey unfolds—an extraordinary narrative positioned not only within the realm of technology but as a fixture of our shared evolutionary story.

Chapter 3

Core Concepts and Technologies

Core concepts and technologies form the backbone of Artificial Intelligence, providing the essential understanding necessary for exploring this complex domain. This chapter delves into the fundamental principles that drive AI frameworks, highlighting key algorithms such as search, optimization, and reasoning strategies. It covers how AI systems represent knowledge and learn through various methodologies, including supervised, unsupervised, and reinforcement learning. By examining the tools and frameworks that facilitate AI development, this chapter equips readers with a comprehensive view of the technological landscape that underpins AI innovation.

3.1 Fundamental Principles of AI

Artificial Intelligence (AI) is the tantalizing dream of creating machines that can think, learn, and adapt with human-like prowess. To explore its fundamental principles, we must first unravel what makes AI tick—a beguiling tapestry woven from strands of logic, mathematics, and creativity. In this section, we embark on a journey through these principles, revealing how they form the bedrock of AI technology.

At the heart of AI lies the concept of *intelligence*, a multi-faceted attribute difficult to pin down. In humans, intelligence encompasses the ability to learn from experience, adapt to new situations, understand complex ideas, and utilize knowledge to manipulate one's environment. AI seeks to endow machines with these abilities, albeit with varied success and in distinct ways. The dawn of AI was inspired by a simple yet profound question: Can machines be made to exhibit such intelligent behaviors?

The story inevitably circles back to Alan Turing, a towering figure in the history of computing and AI. In his seminal 1950 paper, *Computing Machinery and Intelligence*, Turing proposed what has become known as the Turing Test—a criterion for determining a machine's level of intelligence based on its ability to exhibit behavior indistinguishable from that of a human in conversation.

The Turing Test is more than an academic brainteaser; it underscores the importance of *natural language processing* and the quest for machines that can understand and engage in human language—a cornerstone of intelligent behavior. Turing's vision highlighted the principle that intelligence is not solely about raw computation but involves nuanced interaction with the complex human world.

In the early days of AI, pioneering researchers embraced the idea of symbolic AI, which posits that human thought can be represented through the manipulation of symbols, much like language or mathematics. This approach led to the development of rule-based systems, where programmers meticulously encoded expert knowledge into complex networks of *if-then* rules.

Symbolic AI thrives in well-defined domains where

knowledge can be explicitly expressed, such as in chess-playing programs like IBM's Deep Blue, which famously defeated world champion Garry Kasparov in 1997. Here, AI's principle of leveraging structured, expert-driven knowledge shines brightly. Yet, symbolic AI has its constraints, struggling with real-world ambiguity and the vastness of experiential learning.

In recent decades, AI has shifted toward *machine learning*, a paradigm where systems learn from data rather than relying solely on predetermined rules. This shift marks a fundamental principle of AI—the pursuit of generalization from examples. In machine learning, algorithms identify patterns and make decisions based on datasets, allowing for greater adaptability and scope.

Consider facial recognition technology; rather than manually encoding features like eye shape or skin tone, systems train on vast quantities of labeled images, learning to identify faces with astonishing accuracy. This principle of data-driven learning has unlocked new realms of possibility, driving advancements in self-driving cars, language translation, and medical diagnostics.

Machine learning branches into various approaches, the most notable being *supervised learning*, where models are trained on labeled datasets, *unsupervised learning*, which discovers patterns in unlabeled data, and *reinforcement learning*, where agents learn optimal actions through trial and error in dynamic environments.

Central to the modern AI renaissance is deep learning, a subfield of machine learning inspired by the brain's neural architecture. Neural networks, which form the backbone of deep learning, consist of layers of interconnected nodes (akin to neurons), capable of extracting increasingly abstract features from data.

The staggering depth of these networks allows them to

perform tasks previously deemed unattainable by machines. For instance, AI systems can generate realistic images, translate languages with nuance, and best human players in complex games like Go, as demonstrated by DeepMind's AlphaGo.

Yet, this principle of layered abstraction comes with challenges, including the need for vast amounts of data and computational power, plus the elusive "black-box" nature—difficulty in interpreting how decisions are made within these networks.

Another foundational principle of AI is its capacity for reasoning and problem-solving, drawing from logic and mathematics. These capabilities are pivotal in areas such as automated theorem proving, diagnostics, and strategy games.

AI's prowess in reasoning is illustrated by its employment in logistics for optimizing supply chains, in finance for detecting fraudulent transactions, and in healthcare for diagnosing diseases. However, crafting intelligent problem solvers requires a harmonious blend of symbolic reasoning and practical learning methodologies.

Systems like IBM's Watson, which vanquished humans on *Jeopardy!*, showcase AI's potential to amalgamate vast databases of structured and unstructured information, performing complex reasoning to produce accurate and timely solutions.

As we venture deeper into the principles of AI, we encounter the ethical and societal implications of its deployment. AI presents both unprecedented opportunities and profound challenges, from enhancing healthcare to perpetuating biases and displacing jobs.

One principle that emerges is the necessity for *ethical*

AI, driven by fairness, transparency, and accountability. As machines make decisions affecting lives, ensuring responsible AI development is paramount.

Consider an AI system in criminal justice that recommends parole decisions. Such systems must be carefully designed to avoid perpetuating racial or socioeconomic biases. The principle of fairness in AI emphasizes the duty of developers and policymakers to cultivate systems that aspire towards equitable outcomes.

In summary, the fundamental principles of AI form an intricate tapestry that guides its trajectory. From symbolic rule-based systems to the sophistication of neural networks, AI continues to reshape our world in profound ways. As these systems evolve, so too must our understanding of their ethical dimensions, ensuring this double-edged sword yields benefits commensurate with its potential.

In their essence, the principles of AI represent an intersection of mathematics, logic, data, and ethics, ever-evolving to tackle the puzzles of perception, cognition, and interaction in machines. As we conclude this exploration, it becomes evident that the journey of AI is as much about understanding ourselves as it is about mapping intelligence onto machines.

3.2 Key AI Algorithms

Dive into the world of Artificial Intelligence, and you will soon encounter the vibrant hub where key algorithms dance—a place where logic meets creativity, and numbers forge pathways to understanding the universe's most intricate challenges. Here, we explore these algorithms, the hidden engines of AI, that

55

underpin its ability to think, predict, and sometimes even surprise us.

The Beginnings: Search Algorithms

Before the contemporary deluge of data-driven AI, the earliest algorithms were driven by structured search problems. The goal was straightforward yet profound: to explore a space of possibilities to find the best solution. Search algorithms like *breadth-first search* (BFS) and *depth-first search* (DFS) laid the groundwork, navigating decision trees by exploring nodes layer-by-layer or diving into branches, respectively.

Consider a labyrinthine maze. BFS ensures that you explore all corridors closest to your starting point before venturing into deeper recesses, guaranteeing you find the shortest path to your destination if such a path exists. DFS, meanwhile, is akin to a more adventurous pathfinder, delving deep down a path and backtracking only when there's no way forward. Though ancient in the AI realm, these algorithms remain staples, forming the backbone of more sophisticated strategies.

Heuristic Search and the Art of Smart Decision Making

With growing complexity, AI needed more than brute force; it required nuance—the ability to make educated guesses. Enter *heuristics*, rules of thumb that guide search algorithms more efficiently toward promising regions of the solution space. Algorithms like A^* combine a heuristic with path cost, minimizing both the distance already traveled and the expected distance to a goal.

In navigation systems, A^* revolutionizes route planning by estimating the best path before detours, calculating not merely distance but incorporating traffic conditions—

making it a dependable co-pilot in the digital age.

Optimization and the Quest for the Best

When merely finding a solution isn't enough, optimization emerges as the hero. Optimization algorithms seek to improve upon solutions, whether minimizing costs or maximizing outputs. *Gradient descent*, for example, is a cornerstone of machine learning, iterating over mathematical landscapes to find local minima, fostering breakthroughs in areas as diverse as finance, where it reduces investment risks, and in healthcare, optimizing treatment plans.

Another shining star, *genetic algorithms*, mimic natural selection by evolving solutions over successive iterations, or "generations." They exhibit remarkable utility in design and engineering tasks, yielding innovations in antenna configurations for spacecraft where trial and error would be impractical.

Reinforcement Learning: Learning through Rewards

The principles of *reinforcement learning* are reminiscent of training a dog using treats and commands—systems learn optimal actions from consequences rather than explicit instructions. Here, an agent explores its environment, choosing actions that maximize cumulative rewards.

A breathtaking application lies in AlphaGo, the AI system that mastered the complex game of Go. It learned from millions of simulated games, employing reinforcement learning to develop strategies beyond human anticipation. In real-world applications, reinforcement learning optimizes energy consumption in data centers and refines autonomous driving systems, heralding a future where machines dynamically respond to their environments.

Bayesian Networks and Probabilistic Reasoning

In scenarios where uncertainty reigns, *Bayesian networks* shine by modeling probabilistic relationships between variables. Imagine a medical diagnosis system that considers symptoms and potential diseases. Bayesian networks assess the probabilities of various illnesses given observed symptoms, offering refined diagnostic hypotheses.

This approach empowers systems to handle the ambiguity of real-life data, supporting decision-making in contexts like sports analytics, where player performance and injury likelihoods are dynamically assessed, contributing to strategic game plans.

Support Vector Machines and the Power of Margin

A harbinger of precision, *support vector machines* (SVM) revolutionized classification tasks by finding the optimal hyperplane separating data points into distinct classes. By maximizing the margin between data points of different categories, SVM minimizes classification errors—a principle that is especially vital in medical imaging, where it distinguishes between healthy and cancerous tissues with surgical precision.

Neural Networks: The Soul of Deep Learning

Arguably the poster child of modern AI, *neural networks* draw inspiration from the human brain. These multilayered networks of neurons learn complex patterns in visual data, speech, and text. Fueled by vast datasets, they power technologies we use daily, from facial recognition to real-time language translation.

Deep learning, a subset of neural networks, expounded grand advancements in AI capabilities. Applications in natural language processing (NLP) saw machines analyze sentiment, generate human-like text, and unfold narratives in voice-activated assistants like Siri and Alexa.

Despite their prowess, these networks often operate as "black boxes," leading to ongoing research into *interpretability*, ensuring accountability when they partake in critical systems like autonomous vehicles and medical diagnostics.

Generative Adversarial Networks (GANs): Imagination in Algorithms

A more recent marvel is *generative adversarial networks* (GANs), where two neural networks engage in a minuet—one generates data (akin to creating art), and the other discriminates between real and generated data (acting as a critic). This rivalry fosters the creation of increasingly realistic outputs, from uncanny photo-realistic images to immersive virtual environments akin to surreal dreams.

The conduit of creativity, GANs herald potential in art, entertainment, and beyond. Yet, they pose ethical questions about copyright and authenticity, requiring measured guidelines as AI's artistic capabilities expand.

Simulated Annealing and Aspirations of Nature

Mirroring the metal-cooling process of annealing, *simulated annealing* emulates the gradual reduction of thermal excitations to settle in low-energy states. This optimization method seeks globally optimal solutions, with applications in resource allocation and scheduling, where sporadically accepting suboptimal solutions prevents settling into premature conclusions.

Its applications extend to biotechnology, optimizing protein-folding to design proteins with specific functions, outsmarting the evolutionary time needed to achieve therapeutically potent biomolecules.

Algorithmic Philosophies: A Synthesis

While algorithms craft the brain of AI, philosophical reflection forms its conscience. The quest for balance between exploration and exploitation, the reconciliation of efficiency and fairness, and the comprehension of consciousness in machines remain topics of lively discourse.

As we weave through these key algorithms, they reveal an intricate interplay between intuition and rigor, underscoring AI's evolution as a tool that both amplifies human ingenuity and challenges our philosophical understandings. This synthesis of algorithmic and human thinking not only propels decision-making and creativity in novel directions but also demands that we redefine our ethical frameworks and societal norms in harmony with AI's transformative potential.

In sum, the algorithms that constitute AI are the unsung heroes, invisibly enhancing our world one nuanced kick at a time. They frame a future wherein machines, though computationally serendipitous, engage in an epic dialogue with humanity—a conversation capable of igniting imaginations and solving the ultimate enigmas of intelligence itself.

3.3   Representation and Reasoning

In the pursuit of Artificial Intelligence, one key question dominates: how can machines encapsulate the knowledge of the world in a form that allows them to not only understand but also reason about it? Enter the realm of *representation and reasoning*, where AI systems transform information into structured forms that can be manipulated to simulate thinking—an endeavor that stretches back to the earliest aspirations of AI itself.

Symbolic Representation: The Pioneering Efforts

The paradigm of symbolic AI arises from a simple yet profound hypothesis: cognitive processes can be represented through symbolic expressions, much like human language and logic. This premise allowed early AI systems to imitate the way humans solve puzzles, like those familiar logic riddles that start with "If A is true, then B must be..."

In the days of yore, this approach birthed programs capable of playing chess, proving mathematical theorems, and even crafting philosophical arguments—ambitious achievements for their time. A stalwart example is the *Logic Theorist*, developed by Allen Newell and Herbert A. Simon in the 1950s, which elegantly proved mathematical theorems from *Principia Mathematica*, heralding a new dawn for automated reasoning.

Symbolic representation involves encoding concepts of the world using logic-based languages such as *propositional logic* and *predicate calculus*. These languages allow the articulation of facts and relationships in explicit, interpretable terms—"If it rains, the ground gets wet" serves as a canonical prediction, rooted in straightforward truth values.

Frames and Scripts: Scripting Intelligence

Symbolic AI seeks not just to know the truth of isolated propositions, but to weave richer narratives. Enter *frames* and *scripts*, conceptual structures that provide context and order for events and objects, akin to pre-written movie scripts that guide improvisation on stage.

The legendary computer scientist Marvin Minsky introduced the concept of frames in the 1970s, multidimen-

61

sional structures that chunk knowledge into entities and their relationships—think of how you might catalog the intricate characters of a Shakespearean drama.

Meanwhile, scripts, pioneered by Roger Schank in the mid-1970s, succinctly describe sequences of events within common situations, like dining at a restaurant. Machines armed with scripts possess the scaffolding to anticipate events—when offered a menu, they can conjecture that ordering follows, then eating, then paying. This layering upon the scaffolding of reality allows machines to predict outcomes and make decisions based on incomplete information.

Semantic Networks: Weaving the Web of Meaning

Enter the realm of *semantic networks*, graph structures that model knowledge as interconnected nodes and links, akin to the sprawling, intoxicating connections of a detective's evidence board traced back to a scintillating crime scene. Each node encapsulates a concept, and links represent relationships or hierarchies—a visual ontology of knowledge encouraging complex reasoning.

Take, for instance, WordNet, a historical gem of a semantic network that mapped English vocabulary into a web of synonymous sets. Each set interlaces with others through links depicting various lexical relations, giving rise to intricate queries asking not "what is a dog?" but rather "how does 'dog' connect with 'pet,' 'animal,' or 'friend'?"

In information retrieval and natural language processing, semantic networks boost machines' abilities to infer meaning and disambiguate contexts hidden within human utterances, reshaping not just automated customer service but realms like literary analysis—remapping texts into universes of interpretive possibilities.

Production Systems: Rules at Work

Venturing further into the labyrinth of reasoning, *production systems* emerge, driving engines for pattern-directed inference. A production system mirrors the intricate ebb and flow of reasoning—a set of rules ("productions") provides the mechanisms through which the system transitions from one state of being to another, conjuring images of the wizardry of Merlin himself.

These systems comprise three essentials: a global database holding knowledge, a set of condition-action (if-then) rules, and a control system. This triad functions like an orchestra—the database holds music (data), the rules are its scores (instructions), and the control system the maestro, bringing harmony or shifting to crescendo where required.

An intriguing example lies within the architecture of *SOAR*, a general cognitive architecture, which explores learning and problem-solving, demonstrating its prowess across logical game-playing and strategic planning—proving not all AI needs explicit domain knowledge to dance to the music of intelligence, rather it can improvise on the go.

Probabilistic Models: Embracing Uncertainty

From deterministic vistas we traverse to undulating landscapes fringed with uncertainty, where *probabilistic models* come to the fore. These models embrace reality's stochastic nature, equipped to reason under uncertainty through statistical mathematics—a formidable ally when seeking predictions amidst real-world variability.

Bayesian networks, a burgeoning fruit of this principle, encapsulate probabilistic dependencies among variables in a directed acyclic graph. Imagine a physician wielding a Bayesian network to discern likely causes of a set of symptoms, from influenza to rare disorders—probing the unseen with precision.

Probabilistic reasoning extends into speech recognition and natural language processing, offering insight into how machines appraise the ambiguous shuffle of spoken words or penned phrases—rendering spoken word to digital text, unveiling not just words but the music of intention cocooned within them.

Non-monotonic Reasoning: Adapting to New Information

In the dynamic theatre that is life, new evidence often shatters long-held beliefs, leaving us dancing in improvisation—a challenge well met by the artistry of *non-monotonic reasoning*. These systems revamp conclusions in light of new information, eschewing rigid truths for adaptable narratives, echoing the lucidity of human reasoning.

Consider a diagnostic AI suspecting a faulty component in a car engine; new data indicating another malfunction rekindles its deductions. This is not merely a system pulled by logic but one responsive and adaptable, rendering the future nimble and promising.

Real-World Applications: From Theory to Practice

Together, representation and reasoning lay the foundation for vast real-world applications, reaching far beyond libraries and laboratories into the very fabric of our daily lives.

In *legal informatics*, AI systems parse the expansive legal verbiage into actionable logic, providing judges and attorneys with deductive analysis and precedential reasoning, unveiling nuanced arguments in the intricate weave of statutory law.

In the arenas of *smart cities* and *urban planning*, these systems offer dynamic responses to unpredictable variances—traffic patterns, energy flows, emergency responses—crafting safety and efficiency from boundless complexity.

Moreover, envision an imagined future where *AI-driven personal assistants* anticipate needs and automate routines not through rote memorization but nuanced comprehension of individual habits and preferences, facilitating luxuries of time and attention for humanity's creative and introspective pursuits.

Ethical Considerations: Reasoning with Responsibility

Yet, amidst the euphoria of possibilities, one cannot ignore the ethical considerations entwined with AI's growing reach. Ensuring the fidelity of representation and integrity of reasoning calls for conscientious design and regulation.

In fields taut with ethical dilemmas—be it autonomous vehicles making moral decisions, or chatbots navigating complex emotional conversations—AI systems must reflect not just logic but justice, wisdom, and empathy. These are not mere algorithms but mirrors of human values, demanding collaboration between technologists, ethicists, and society itself.

Conclusion: The Continuum of Cognition

In sum, representation and reasoning are the dual heart-beat of AI—a testament to humanity's quest to imbue machines with the cognizance of thought, adaptable yet anchored in science. They whisper the possibility not merely of mere mimicry but of partnership, where humans and machines coalesce into harmonized synergy.

In this interplay, new narratives unravel, fueling curiosities and illuminating paths uncharted. The future, it seems, is not automated but collaborated—a testament to the intertwined destinies of minds and machines on the ever-evolving continuum of cognition.

3.4   Learning in AI Systems

Imagine a painter faced with a blank canvas, each brushstroke enhancing the complexity of the masterpiece, until a stunning image emerges that captures both the mind and the heart. Such is the essence of learning in Artificial Intelligence (AI) systems—a dance of data and algorithms producing insights that once seemed exclusive to the realm of human intellect. In this section, we explore the various facets of learning in AI, tracing its evolution and its profound impact on our world.

The Genesis of Machine Learning

In the early days of AI, machines were programmed with explicit instructions—a symphony orchestrated by human composers. However, with the advent of machine learning (ML), AI systems began to compose tunes of their own. Machine learning is a branch of AI that endows machines with the ability to improve their performance through experience, akin to a budding chef refining recipes through countless tastings.

The journey began in earnest in the mid-20th century, with pioneers like Arthur Samuel, who famously defined machine learning as the "field of study that gives computers the ability to learn without being explicitly programmed." Samuel's work on a checkers-playing program marked a milestone, demonstrating that a machine could learn strategies by playing against itself.

Supervised Learning: Guided by Labeled Examples

At the heart of machine learning lies *supervised learning*, a method that relies on labeled datasets to train models. Supervised learning is akin to a student learning under the watchful eye of a teacher, where each lesson is accompanied by examples with correct answers.

Consider a system trained to recognize images of cats and dogs. In supervised learning, the model ingests vast datasets of images, each labeled as "cat" or "dog." The model learns to associate particular features—like whiskers or floppy ears—with each category and refines its predictions over time.

Supervised learning permeates numerous real-world applications. In healthcare, it's used to identify diseases from medical images, while in finance, it powers fraud detection systems. These applications underscore supervised learning's ability to derive meaningful patterns from labeled data, fostering an era where AI assists in critical decision-making across industries.

Unsupervised Learning: Discovering Hidden Patterns

While supervised learning provides clear guidance, *unsupervised learning* ventures into the unknown, seeking to discover hidden structures within unlabeled data. It's akin to an explorer venturing into uncharted territory, finding patterns without pre-existing maps.

Unsupervised learning is exemplified by *clustering algorithms*, which group data into clusters based on similarity. Imagine sorting a pile of seashells by shape and hue without prior knowledge—unsupervised learning identifies the natural groupings within the chaos.

Applications abound, from customer segmentation in marketing, which tailors personalized experiences, to anomaly detection in security, identifying network intrusions or fraudulent transactions without prior examples. This ability to reveal insights without labels makes unsupervised learning an invaluable tool in exploratory data analysis.

Reinforcement Learning: Learning from Interaction

At the frontier of AI's learning capabilities lies *reinforcement learning* (RL), a method inspired by theories of behavioral psychology. In RL, agents learn by interacting with their environment, receiving feedback in the form of rewards or penalties—the AI equivalent of a child learning not to touch a hot stove after a painful encounter.

Reinforcement learning has paved the way for breakthroughs in dynamic decision-making environments. Consider the game of Go, renowned for its complexity, where RL enabled DeepMind's AlphaGo to defeat a world champion, demonstrating strategic ingenuity surpassing human expertise.

Beyond games, RL finds applications in self-driving cars, where AI must make real-time decisions based on ever-changing road conditions, and in robotic systems, which adapt to new tasks through trial and error—a testament to machines not just following instructions but synthesizing strategies in real-world settings.

Neural Networks and Deep Learning: The Architects of

Perception

Central to the recent renaissance in machine learning are *neural networks*, a class of models inspired by the neural architecture of the human brain. These models consist of layers of interconnected nodes (neurons) that transform input data into output predictions, much like how neurons in the brain process sensory information.

Deep learning—using neural networks with many layers—propelled AI to new heights, enabling machines to learn directly from raw data. A neural network trained on images, for instance, can autonomously identify intricate features, such as the curves of a cat's tail or patterns in raindrops, without prescribed rules.

Deep learning has unlocked transformative applications, from voice assistants like Siri and Alexa understanding speech, to autonomous vehicles interpreting visual scenes. Yet, the power of neural networks also introduces challenges, such as the need for large datasets and computational resources, and the enigma of their "black box" nature, where the reasons behind a decision are often obscured.

Transfer Learning: Learning from the Past

Traditional models often require extensive labeled datasets, but *transfer learning* offers a shortcut by leveraging knowledge from one domain to accelerate learning in another. It's as if a seasoned violinist took up the cello, using established musical skills to learn a new instrument efficiently.

Transfer learning gained prominence with the rise of deep learning, where pre-trained models can be adapted to new tasks with minimal data. In image recognition, models pre-trained on vast datasets, like ImageNet, can be fine-tuned to identify specific objects, such as distinguishing between various species of birds.

This approach not only reduces the need for data and computational resources but also extends AI's reach to niche applications previously constrained by data scarcity—efforts as diverse as detecting specific diseases in medical imaging to cataloging rare wildlife species from photographs.

Challenges and Ethical Considerations in AI Learning

As AI systems expand their capabilities, they also raise important ethical and societal questions regarding bias, privacy, and accountability. AI models, particularly in supervised learning, can inadvertently learn discriminatory patterns if trained on biased data, perpetuating and amplifying injustices inadvertently woven into training datasets.

These ethical landscapes demand rigorous scrutiny and conscientious designs, ensuring equity and security. Efforts like *explainable AI* strive to illuminate the decision-making within AI systems, fostering transparency and trust in critical domains like healthcare and justice.

Moreover, the rise of AI learning imparts societal transformations—altering job markets, sparking debates on data ownership, and challenging traditional paradigms of creativity and intellect. Ensuring positive outcomes requires an inclusive dialogue encompassing technologists, policymakers, ethicists, and the public.

The Future of Learning in AI

As we stand on the cusp of AI's expansive horizon, learning remains at the heart of its promise—a force driving machines toward accomplishing feats once relegated to the annals of science fiction. Each stride forward in AI learning marks progress not just in technology but in our understanding of intelligence itself.

Looking ahead, advancements in learning algorithms promise to bolster AI's adaptability, robustness, and interpretability. Pioneering efforts in *self-supervised learning* seek to balance the structured approach of supervised learning with the spontaneity of unsupervised methods, allowing AI to grasp underlying structures in data with minimal human intervention.

Moreover, efforts in *lifelong learning* envision systems that continuously learn and adapt throughout their existence, much like humans, culminating in AI's ability to integrate knowledge, adapt to new situations, and perhaps one day converse about art, philosophy, or compassion—an AI as a collaborator in the human journey, rather than a mere tool.

The narrative of learning in AI is an ongoing tale of discovery and innovation, where every advance brings with it challenges and new insights into the fabric of understanding. As AI continues to evolve, it not only alters the landscape of technology but also promises to profoundly enrich the tapestry of human experience, weaving threads of innovation and curiosity with those of wisdom and ethics to create a future of shared potential.

3.5 Tools and Frameworks

The efficacy of an artist often lies in the tools they wield, and the realm of Artificial Intelligence (AI) is no different. With AI's rapid evolution, a vibrant ecosystem of tools and frameworks has emerged as vital enablers, transforming abstract theories and algorithms into world-altering applications. In this section, we embark on a tour through this ecosystem, uncovering how these instruments of innovation empower scientists,

71

developers, and everyone in between to push the boundaries of what's possible.

The Historical Tapestry: From Code to Application

To appreciate the modern AI toolkit, it's enlightening to glance back at its roots. Early AI researchers were akin to pioneers venturing into uncharted technological territories, crafting foundational tools from scratch—formulating code directly on mainframes with limited resources. These rudimentary, homegrown solutions set the stage for future tools designed to mimic human cognition through logic and reasoning.

As AI matured, programming languages like LISP and Prolog surfaced, tailored for symbolic reasoning. LISP, in particular, became the lingua franca of AI research, thanks to its aptitude for symbolic processing. These languages, though esoteric, sparked a revolution in automated reasoning, laying the groundwork for today's sophisticated AI frameworks and tools.

Python: The Lingua Franca of Modern AI

Enter Python—a versatile, high-level programming language now synonymous with AI development. Python's ascendancy is no accident; its readability, simplicity, and vast ecosystem of libraries make it the ideal choice for AI practitioners.

Python's libraries have become key players in the AI scene. For instance, *NumPy* and *Pandas* facilitate data manipulation and analysis, while *SciPy* offers scientific computing prowess. These libraries streamline handling large datasets—a necessity for training AI models.

Moreover, *Matplotlib* and *Seaborn* enable visualizations,

allowing researchers to graphically interpret data, spanning from the mundane to the marvelous. The combination of these tools forms an indispensable foundation for data scientists, assisting in cleaning, analyzing, and visualizing data with remarkable efficiency.

TensorFlow and PyTorch: Titans of Deep Learning

In deep learning, two frameworks dominate: *TensorFlow* and *PyTorch*. These behemoths have revolutionized how neural networks are built, trained, and deployed.

Launched by Google's Brain team, TensorFlow is acclaimed for its flexibility and scalability, supporting an array of operations—from research prototyping to running production-grade models at industrial scales. TensorFlow's versatility is further exemplified by *Keras*, its high-level API, which simplifies neural network construction through user-friendly abstractions.

Meanwhile, PyTorch, developed by Facebook's AI Research lab, has gained popularity for its dynamic computation graph, resembling Pythonic idioms. This feature makes PyTorch particularly appealing for researchers who value experimental fluidity, allowing seamless modifications and immediate execution—a haven for those in academia and research-focused arenas.

Between them, TensorFlow and PyTorch power a vast array of applications: from autonomous vehicles interpreting 3D environments to healthcare AI diagnosing illnesses from medical images. Their impact is undeniable, each stride built upon the shoulders of these frameworks.

Scikit-Learn: The Swiss Army Knife of Classical Machine Learning

While deep learning garners much fanfare, it's essential to remember the bedrock of classical machine learning, supported by *Scikit-Learn*. This library stands as a paragon for implementing supervised and unsupervised learning methods with grace and simplicity.

Scikit-Learn harmonizes an assortment of algorithms— linear regression, k-means clustering, decision trees— offering elegant interfaces to build models, tune hyperparameters, and assess performance through a golden standard of cross-validation. In practical scenarios, it acts as the Swiss Army knife for swift iterations across datasets, elucidating hidden patterns and predictions.

Deployed in various sectors, from economic forecasting to biotech analytics, Scikit-Learn exemplifies the potency of classical approaches when data structures conform to traditional paradigms, offering transparency in an era dominated by neural networks' opaque decisions.

Jupyter Notebooks: Interactive Storyboarding for Data Science

Jupyter Notebooks have transcended their technical confines to become narrative tools for data storytelling. A testament to open-source collaboration, they host an interactive computational environment where code, text, and visuals coalesce.

Jupyter Notebooks enable researchers to document workflows, conduct exploratory data analysis, and share insights with clarity, serving as both a laboratory and a publishing platform. They democratize data science by transforming analysis from a solitary task to a collaborative endeavor, with richly annotated notebooks illuminating the rationale behind each decision.

Companies and universities alike leverage Jupyter Notebooks for reproducible research and pedagogy, ensuring that findings are transparent, interpretable, and, crucially, shareable—a critical facet in the digital age.

Docker: Containerizing the AI Revolution

Docker enters the fray as a pivotal ally in deploying AI models. As code crosses from development to production, discrepancies in environmental configurations can lead to maddening inconsistencies—a problem resolved by Docker's containerization.

Docker encapsulates applications and their dependencies in self-contained units or containers, ensuring consistent execution across any environment. This reliability is indispensable for AI solutions needing deployment into complex infrastructures like cloud services or edge devices.

Moreover, Docker's orchestration tools, like Kubernetes, simplify scaling AI applications in response to fluctuating demands. In essence, Docker empowers practitioners to transform prototypes into production-grade solutions that traverse the globe, accelerating AI's ubiquity.

Ethical Considerations in AI Tool Development

As we forge ahead with AI tools and frameworks, it's crucial to address the ethical dimensions implicit in their design and deployment. Tool creators wield significant influence, dictating the capabilities and limitations of AI applications, necessitating a conscientious approach.

Ensuring fairness, transparency, and accessibility in AI tools becomes paramount—for biased datasets and opaque algorithms can perpetuate or exacerbate societal inequities. Explorations in *ethical AI* guide practitioners to audit models for imbalances, advocating for inclusivity and equity in tool development.

Moreover, responsibly curating datasets, documenting decision rationales, and implementing rigorous testing procedures are essential practices in creating tools that not only enhance technology but also resonate with societal values.

The Collaborative Future of AI Tools and Frameworks

The future of AI's tools and frameworks promises even greater collaborative synergy, heralding platforms that integrate diverse aspects of AI development into holistic ecosystems. These all-encompassing environments aspire to streamline workflows, from data ingestion to model deployment, marrying varied technologies into seamless pipelines.

Emerging ideas in *low-code* and *no-code* AI platforms invite a broader audience to participate in AI development, lowering barriers for non-programmers to engage in creating AI solutions through intuitive interfaces. This democratization holds immense potential for cross-disciplinary innovations, incorporating insights from fields traditionally outside the technological sphere.

Moreover, the advancements in AI are inextricably linked to the continued efforts in building robust frameworks that prioritize ethical standards. Research in explainable and fair AI promises to imbue future tools with the transparency and accountability required for responsible usage.

Conclusion: A Symphony of Innovation

The landscape of AI tools and frameworks resembles a dynamic symphony—an intricate orchestration where each instrument contributes to a harmonious whole. It is this collective ensemble that empowers engineers and scientists to not only dream bigger but translate those dreams into reality, crafting solutions that redefine industries and improve lives.

As AI continues to mature, the tools and frameworks at our disposal will undoubtedly evolve, reflecting the needs, aspirations, and values of societies embracing intelligent technology. By meticulously tending to both the technical and ethical facets of this evolution, we ensure a future where AI acts as a catalyst for positive change, harmonizing with human endeavors to create a more insightful, equitable, and prosperous world.

Chapter 4

Machine Learning and Its Applications

Machine learning is a critical component of Artificial Intelligence that enables systems to learn from data and improve over time without explicit programming. This chapter explores the different types of machine learning, including supervised, unsupervised, and reinforcement learning, providing insights into their distinct methodologies and use cases. It discusses a variety of algorithms and models, such as decision trees and neural networks, that form the basis of machine learning applications. By examining real-world implementations across diverse sectors, it reveals both the vast potential and the challenges inherent in deploying machine learning technologies.

4.1   Understanding Machine Learning

Machine learning, a term that has become almost synonymous with modern technological advancement, is a fascinating branch of artificial intelligence. It is, at its core, a method of teaching computers to learn from data and to improve their performance over time without being explicitly programmed for specific tasks. This ability of machines to adapt and evolve in response to new information has profound implications for virtually every field of human endeavor, from healthcare to finance, transportation, and beyond.

To truly understand machine learning, one must first appreciate the distinction between traditional programming and the paradigm introduced by machine learning. In conventional programming, a human developer writes explicit instructions that tell a computer how to perform a task. This approach works well for straightforward problems: add two numbers, spell-check a document, or sort a list. However, it quickly becomes impractical for more complex tasks like recognizing a face in an image or translating a language. This is where machine learning steps in to bridge the gap.

At its essence, machine learning involves feeding large amounts of data into algorithms, which then discern patterns or relationships within this data. These algorithms can be thought of as mathematical models, albeit with the sophistication to adjust their own parameters based on feedback from the data they encounter. This self-adjusting feature enables machine learning systems to make predictions or decisions without being specifically designed for those exact scenarios.

Consider a simple analogy: training a dog. Initially, you might tell the dog to "sit" and reward it when it correctly follows the command. Over time, the dog learns to associate the word "sit" with sitting down because it has learned from the outcomes (the rewards). Similarly, in supervised machine learning, an algorithm learns from labeled data — data that includes both the input and the desired output — and adjusts itself to improve performance based on the outcomes.

The origins of machine learning can be traced back to the mid-20th century, though its intellectual roots stretch even further back. Early computers were cumbersome, performing only the most elementary calculations. The concept of machine learning gained traction as researchers aspired to create machines that could mimic human learning and thinking. In 1959, Arthur Samuel, a pioneer in artificial intelligence, coined the term "machine learning" in the context of a computer program that improved its performance playing checkers, learning from mistakes and honing its strategy game after game.

Despite these early advances, genuine progress in machine learning was stagnant for several decades, primarily due to limitations in data and computing power. However, the exponential growth of the internet and advancements in hardware during the late 20th and early 21st centuries provided an abundance of data and the means to process it efficiently. This catapulted machine learning from being a largely theoretical concept to a practical tool with a plethora of applications.

Understanding the transformation brought on by machine learning involves examining its various types and purposes. One main type of machine learning is supervised learning, where the system is trained on a labeled dataset, meaning that each training example is paired with an input/output example. The goal of supervised learning is to predict the output of new, unseen instances based on the patterns it has learned. For example, a supervised learning algorithm might be trained with a set of images labeled "cat" or "not cat" and tasked with identifying new photos correctly.

In contrast, unsupervised learning deals with unlabeled data. Here, the machine must find hidden patterns or intrinsic structures without reference to known labels. This approach is often used for clustering similar items or discovering associations between variables. Think of unsupervised learning as akin to a tourist in a foreign land trying to group menu items into categories based on visual similarity and occasional tastings, rather than on explicit instructions from a guidebook.

Another intriguing branch of machine learning is reinforcement learning, inspired by behavioral psychology. Here, an algorithm learns to complete a task by seeking to maximize some notion of cumulative reward. It operates in an environment where it must make a series of decisions, each affecting its ultimate goal: optimizing the reward. This type is well-suited to tasks like game playing or robotic movements, where sequential actions can vastly impact the outcome.

Machine learning, however, is not a perfect science. It comes with its own set of challenges and limitations. For one, the quality and quantity of data are critical to the success of this endeavor. "Garbage in, garbage out" is a common maxim, emphasizing that poor-quality data inevitably leads to poor-quality models. Furthermore, machine learning algorithms can perpetuate biases present in the training data, leading to unfair or discriminatory outcomes. This issue is becoming increasingly important as machine learning systems are integrated into sensitive areas like criminal justice and recruitment.

Moreover, while machines are excellent at identifying patterns in vast datasets, they still lack contextual understanding. Unlike humans, they don't possess innate common sense or the ability to reason abstractly—at least not yet. Thus, while a machine might be able to recommend books based on past reading habits, it may not anticipate the human desire for novelty or surprise.

Despite these challenges, machine learning offers unprecedented opportunities to create smarter, more innovative tech solutions. In healthcare, it provides intelligent systems capable of diagnosing diseases from medical images with remarkable accuracy. In transportation, it underpins the development of autonomous vehicles that promise safer and more efficient travel. Financial services utilize machine learning algorithms to detect fraud more swiftly and accurately than a human could.

As machine learning continues to evolve, its impact on society will only grow. It invites a reevaluation of what it means to learn and understand, both for humans and machines. While machines might excel at certain tasks, they are still part of a larger ecosystem of human creativity and judgement. Understanding machine learning, therefore, is not just about comprehending a set of algorithms, but appreciating its broader implications for our world—a world that is becoming increasingly interconnected and intelligent by design.

4.2 Types of Machine Learning

Machine learning, like any intriguing tale of discovery, unfolds through the exploration of variety. At the heart of this technological renaissance lie three principal types of machine learning: supervised learning, unsupervised learning, and reinforcement learning. Each of these represents a distinct pathway that machines tread, each with its own unique strategies, applications, and charms.

Supervised Learning: The Guided Approach

Imagine yourself a painter, learning under the careful watch of a seasoned mentor. You are given a scene to replicate and receive feedback on each brushstroke. This is akin to supervised learning, where an algorithm learns from a labeled dataset—a collection of input-output pairs—to predict outcomes for new, unseen data. The objective here is to infer a mapping from inputs to the desired outputs, utilizing past knowledge as a guide.

The conceptual roots of supervised learning can be traced back to mathematical models and statistical methods long before the advent of digital computing. These foundational ideas form the backdrop for modern supervised learning algorithms like linear regression, logistic regression, and decision trees. Over time, these methodologies have evolved, leveraging ever-growing reservoirs of data and computational power.

A quintessential application of supervised learning is in image classification. Consider the task of training a machine to distinguish between pictures of cats and dogs. By exposing the algorithm to a vast number of labeled images — some tagged "cat" and others "dog" — the machine learns to identify patterns and features characteristic of each animal. Upon encountering a new image, the machine uses its learned model to predict whether the image is more likely to be a cat or a dog.

Supervised learning shines in areas such as fraud detection, where models can be trained using historical transaction data to identify patterns indicative of fraudulent activity. Moreover, in the medical domain, supervised learning models are employed to predict the onset of diseases by analyzing patient data, enabling earlier interventions and improved patient outcomes.

Unsupervised Learning: The Autonomous Explorer

Step into the shoes of an explorer, wandering a new continent without a map, piecing together fragmented landscapes into a coherent mosaic. Unsupervised learning captures this essence of discovery without explicit guidance, seeking to unravel hidden patterns and structures in data devoid of labels.

This type of machine learning is particularly suited to tasks like clustering, where the aim is to group similar items together. Consider the colossal volumes of data generated by social media platforms, filled with countless voices expressing diverse opinions. Unsupervised learning algorithms utilize clustering to identify distinct communities or interest groups within this chaotic data space, enabling more targeted advertising strategies or sentiment analysis.

Unsupervised learning also finds application in dimensionality reduction, a process analogous to distilling a sprawling epic into a succinct narrative. Techniques such as Principal Component Analysis (PCA) reduce the complexity of data while retaining its essential features, thereby enhancing the efficiency of subsequent data processing tasks. This is particularly useful in fields like genomics, where high-dimensional data can hinder direct analysis.

Among the more intriguing uses of unsupervised learning is anomaly detection. Systems for monitoring network security can discern irregular patterns of network traffic, flagging potential breaches before they escalate into major security incidents.

Reinforcement Learning: Learning through Trial and Error

Imagine a child learning to ride a bicycle, wobbling, tipping over, and trying again. Through trial and error, they gradually learn to balance and steer. Reinforcement learning embodies this spirit of experiential learning, where algorithms learn optimal behaviors within an environment by interacting with it and receiving feedback in the form of rewards or penalties.

Rooted in behavioral psychology, reinforcement learning is reminiscent of how creatures adapt to their surroundings. It has gained prominence in areas such as robotics, where it enables machines to master complex tasks like navigating cluttered environments or manipulating objects — tasks that are remarkably difficult to encode with rule-based programming.

The principles of reinforcement learning are also used in game-playing AI, with notable examples like AlphaGo, which famously defeated the human world champion in the ancient game of Go. Here, the AI learned over millions of simulated games, developing increasingly sophisticated strategies through a process called deep reinforcement learning, which combines reinforcement learning with neural networks.

Self-driving cars offer another exciting application of reinforcement learning. These vehicles continuously learn from their surroundings, making split-second decisions to navigate safely and efficiently. By processing vast amounts of sensor data, they adjust to complex traffic environments, balancing the dual objectives of reaching destinations and minimizing risks.

The Broader Implications

While each type of machine learning offers its own narrative of discovery and innovation, the interplay between them should not be overlooked. In many real-world scenarios, solutions are crafted by combining elements from different kinds of learning. Semi-supervised learning, for instance, sits at the intersection of supervised and unsupervised paradigms, utilizing small amounts of labeled data alongside vast quantities of unlabeled data to enhance learning efficiency.

Moreover, the boundaries of machine learning types are constantly being redefined as new methodologies emerge and existing ones are refined. Transfer learning allows a model trained on one task to be repurposed for another, minimizing the need for extensive retraining and opening up new vistas of opportunity.

Challenges and Considerations

Each type of machine learning is accompanied by its own set of challenges and considerations. For supervised learning, the need for large datasets with accurate labels can be prohibitive, while unsupervised learning might struggle with high-dimensional datasets where patterns are subtle or elusive. Reinforcement learning, on the other hand, demands a delicate balance between exploration and exploitation — exploring new strategies while optimizing known ones.

Ethical considerations also play a significant role. Machine learning systems, regardless of type, are not immune to biases introduced by their training data or how they are deployed. Caution must be exercised to ensure that these powerful tools are used responsibly, maintaining fairness and transparency.

Understanding the types of machine learning opens a window into the multifaceted world of artificial intelligence. These types are more than just technical methodologies — they are stories of persistence, discovery, and innovation. As we continue to develop and apply these remarkable technologies, a broader understanding will foster not only more intelligent machines but also more thoughtful applications, benefiting society as a whole. Through careful stewardship, the capabilities of machine learning can be harnessed to create a future where AI complements human ingenuity and potential.

4.3 Algorithms and Models

In the world of machine learning, algorithms and models are the unsung heroes quietly performing the heavy lifting. If machine learning were an orchestra, algorithms and models would be the musicians interpreting the notes (data) into a beautiful symphony of insights. They transform raw, unstructured information into structured and actionable predictions, classifications, and decisions. But how do these algorithms and models achieve such feats? Let's explore their intricate world through accessible analogies, a touch of history, and practical applications.

The Algorithmic Foundation: Tools of the Trade

The term "algorithm" may sound intimidating, but in reality, it is a step-by-step procedure, akin to a recipe, which guides computers in making sense of data. Algorithms process inputs, draw patterns, and produce outputs that empower decision-making. Machine learning relies on a multitude of algorithms, each crafted for specific types of tasks.

One of the simplest and oldest algorithms is linear regression, a mathematical wizardry used to predict outcomes based on the relationship between variables. Picture yourself trying to predict the price of a house based on its size. A linear regression algorithm attempts to draw the line of best fit through data points of house size versus price, thus allowing predictions for unseen homes.

Moving from the straightforward to the sophisticated, decision trees come into the limelight. They resemble flowcharts, where data is split into branches based on feature values, leading to decision nodes and outcomes. Decision trees capture the essence of a flowchart—a visual representation of decisions and their possible consequences—making them intuitive yet powerful tools for classification tasks. They operate like a series of yes-no questions leading to a decision; think of it as a game of 20 Questions guiding you to guess the right object.

While linear regression and decision trees lay the groundwork, the realm of machine learning really gets exciting with algorithms like support vector machines (SVM) and neural networks. Support vector machines are the perfectionists of classification, drawing the optimal boundary—or hyperplane—that divides data into distinct groups. If you imagine data as dots on a page, SVMs ensure that there's a wide margin separating these groups, maximizing the separation between categories while remaining elegant and precise.

Neural Networks: The Imitation Game

Neural networks are the pièce de résistance in the world of machine learning models. Inspired by the human brain, these structures mimic the way neurons communicate with each other through layers that process intricate patterns. A neural network consists of layers of nodes, each taking inputs, applying transformations, and passing outputs to subsequent layers—a process analogous to a relay race where the baton is passed from one runner to the next, each contributing to the final outcome.

The conceptual origins of neural networks can be traced back to the 1940s, but it wasn't until the mid-1980s that they gained traction. The subsequent explosion of interest in neural networks is tied to developments like backpropagation, a learning algorithm that enables networks to adjust their internal weights and biases through iteratively comparing predictions against known outputs.

In practical terms, neural networks demonstrate their prowess through applications like image and speech recognition. They fuel the technology in your smartphone that unlocks through facial recognition or transcribes voice commands into text. A landmark achievement, which captured the world's imagination, was when neural networks allowed computers to identify objects in images with near-human accuracy during the ImageNet competition—a yearly event where algorithms compete to recognize items from a defined list of categories.

Models in Action: The Art of Generalization

While algorithms provide the mechanics, models are the embodiments of learned knowledge. They are the unique expressions of behavior crafted from data and algorithms, responsible for making predictions or finding patterns. In machine learning parlance, a model can be thought of as a trained mathematical representation inferred from the training dataset.

A good model should not merely memorize past data— it must generalize well to novel, unseen instances. The balance between learning from the data and being able to apply that learning broadly is pivotal. Imagine you're learning to bake cookies—your success hinges upon understanding not only how to follow a recipe but adapting to varying oven temperatures or ingredient substitutions. A robust machine learning model similarly needs to be flexible and adaptive, possessing a finely-tuned balance between underfitting (a model too simple to capture the nuances) and overfitting (a model too complex and thus prone to error when faced with new data).

Take for instance, ensemble learning, a strategy that uses

multiple algorithms or models to enhance performance. Ensembles such as random forests—a collection of decision trees—effectively reduce errors by leveraging the diversity within its individual elements. This diversity results in more stable predictions, much like how a panel of diverse judges might yield a more balanced verdict than any single voice.

A Historical Interlude: From Minsky to Miracles

The journey from early machine learning models to today's sophisticated networks and ensembles has been fraught with challenges and triumphs. Marvin Minsky's work in the mid-20th century laid the foundational understanding of neural networks but faced limitations. In fact, the AI winter of the 1970s and 1980s—a period characterized by reduced funding and interest—came partly due to difficulties in hardware and algorithmic development.

However, the dawn of the 21st century saw a renaissance in AI and machine learning. The computational power needed to train complex models became available, and large-scale datasets provided the fertile ground needed for growth. Breakthroughs in deep learning—complex neural networks with many layers—exemplified by innovations like convolutional and recurrent neural networks, revolutionized areas such as natural language processing and autonomous driving.

Today's machine learning success stories are built upon the shoulders of giants who navigated early skepticism. The realization of self-driving cars, augmented reality, and automated diagnosis would have been science fiction mere decades ago. Yet, these are now practical realities thanks to the robust frameworks forged by cumulative innovations in algorithms and models.

The Challenges: Navigating the Maze

Despite their transformative potential, algorithms and models are not without challenges. The opacity of complex neural networks—the so-called "black box" problem—complicates their interpretability. This can lead to difficulties in understanding their decision-making processes, raising ethical and practical concerns especially in areas with significant societal impact like healthcare or criminal justice.

Moreover, the substantial computational resources required for training sophisticated models, coupled with the need for vast amounts of labeled data, presents logistical constraints. Addressing these challenges requires innovative approaches such as federated learning, which enables model training across decentralized devices while maintaining data privacy—a particularly significant endeavor in a world increasingly concerned with data governance and privacy.

Conclusion: Algorithms and Models as Catalysts of Change

In their myriad forms, algorithms and models represent the epitome of the machine learning movement, seamlessly translating vast seas of data into actionable intelligence. They embody the pursuit of knowledge and the transformation of the theoretical into the tangible, turning pages of theories into the tools that shape our daily interactions with technology. As we advance further into the digital age, the role of these algorithms and models as catalysts for innovation and change will only become more pronounced, illuminating paths to extraordinary futures yet imagined.

4.4 Real-World Applications

Machine learning, once the playground of ivory tower academics and visionary tech aficionados, has leapt from the pages of science fiction to the core of our everyday existence. Like a quietly competent orchestra, it plays in the background, harmonizing various facets of our lives—from the mundane to the majestic. Think of it as the invisible hand steering newer, smarter, and more efficient systems, transforming industries with a subtle but profound touch.

Healthcare: Diagnostics and Beyond

One of the most profound impacts of machine learning is seen in the realm of healthcare. Imagine a future where diseases are diagnosed with pinpoint accuracy, treatments are tailored to individual genetic profiles, and out-of-hospital monitoring can predict health crises before they occur. This is not a distant dream but an emerging reality, largely thanks to machine learning.

Machine learning algorithms analyze medical images—such as X-rays, MRIs, and CT scans—to identify conditions such as tumors with a precision that rivals or exceeds that of experienced radiologists. They detect patterns and anomalies that might escape the human eye, offering early diagnosis and thereby increasing the effectiveness of treatments. In fact, recent advancements have seen AI systems diagnosing specific types of cancer and retinopathy with remarkable accuracy.

Beyond diagnostics, machine learning supports personalized medicine. By analyzing genetic information and other biological data, algorithms help determine which treatments will be most effective for individual patients, minimizing trial and error in medication selection. These tailored approaches significantly enhance the efficacy of treatments, particularly in chronic conditions and cancers.

Moreover, wearable health monitors integrated with machine learning algorithms offer real-time health insights. These devices track vital signs, physical activity, and sleep patterns, alerting users and healthcare providers to potential health issues. Thus, machine learning acts as an ever-watchful guardian, subtly guiding personal health management.

Finance: On the Money

In the world of finance, machine learning is akin to a savvy investor, making sense of oceans of data to identify trends, manage risk, and prevent fraud. Algorithms analyze stock market data, economic indicators, and news feeds to predict market movements. These predictions empower investors to make informed decisions, akin to crystal balls revealing glimpses of financial futures.

Fraud detection is another area where machine learning shines. With the rise of digital transactions, the need for robust fraud prevention systems is paramount. Machine learning analyzes transaction patterns, identifying anomalies that deviate from the norm. This allows for real-time fraud detection, protecting both consumers and financial institutions. Imagine getting a notification when an unusual purchase is detected on your credit card—often thanks to a machine learning algorithm working tirelessly in the background.

Risk management in banking and insurance is also enhanced by machine learning. Algorithms assess the likelihood of defaulting loans, enabling banks to adjust interest rates and lending policies accordingly. This not only safeguards financial institutions but also contributes to systemic stability in the financial ecosystem.

Transportation: The Road Ahead

In transportation, machine learning is steering us towards a safer, more efficient future. Autonomous vehicles, once the stuff of imagination, are now a burgeoning reality. By processing data from sensors and cameras, autonomous driving systems can navigate roads, obey traffic rules, and make split-second decisions to avoid collisions. This intelligent adaptability reduces accidents and promises to revolutionize personal and commercial transportation.

Public transport systems benefit too, with machine learning optimizing routes and schedules based on real-time data. Imagine predictive models that adjust train or bus schedules in response to passenger patterns, minimizing waiting times and enhancing commuter convenience.

In the logistics sector, machine learning optimizes supply chain operations. Algorithms predict demand, manage inventory, and streamline routes for delivery trucks, reducing costs and improving efficiency. This seamless orchestration ensures that goods flow smoothly from manufacturers to consumers, reminiscent of a well-conducted symphony, where each part plays its role in perfect harmony.

Retail: The Consumer Connection

In retail, machine learning acts as both guide and companion, enhancing the customer experience at every touchpoint. Personalized recommendations have become the norm—when you browse shopping websites or streaming services, machine learning algorithms suggest products or shows you might like, based on your previous interactions.

These recommendation systems are powered by analyzing vast amounts of data, detecting preferences, predicting behavior, and tailoring recommendations to individual tastes. It's akin to having a personal shopping assistant, one that knows your style better than your wardrobe does.

Furthermore, machine learning is transforming inventory management. Predictive analytics forecast demand for products, helping retailers maintain optimal stock levels and reduce waste. This not only keeps customers satisfied with ready availability but also enhances the sustainability of supply chains.

Entertainment: A New Stage

The entertainment industry has embraced machine learning with open arms, utilizing its capabilities to thrill and captivate audiences. In film and music production, machine learning algorithms analyze vast data sets to predict audience preferences and optimize content delivery. Your favorite films are likely suggested through clever algorithms, which also guide content creation, ensuring it aligns with prevailing trends.

Moreover, in esports and video games, machine learning enhances player experience. AI-driven opponents provide tailored challenges, adjusting their difficulty based on player skill, ensuring engagement without frustration. This intelligent customization makes gaming a more immersive and rewarding pastime.

Agriculture: Cultivating Efficiency

Even in the age-old practice of agriculture, machine learning is sowing seeds of innovation. Precision agriculture leverages machine learning to optimize inputs like water, fertilizers, and pesticides, ensuring their efficient use while maximizing yields. Algorithms analyze soil health, weather patterns, and crop conditions to guide decision-making.

Drone technology, paired with machine learning, inspects vast fields, identifying areas requiring attention with pinpoint accuracy. This reduces labor costs, enhances crop health, and promotes sustainable farming practices. It's an impressive convergence of technology and tradition—resulting in higher productivity with less environmental impact.

The Promise and the Paradox

The applications of machine learning are as vast as they are varied. From healthcare to agriculture, finance to entertainment, machine learning offers profound solutions to complex problems. Yet, its widespread adoption invites closer scrutiny concerning ethical use and societal impact.

The paradox of machine learning lies in its potential to both empower and displace. Automation streamlines processes but raises concerns about job displacement. As machines evolve to execute tasks more efficiently, human roles must also evolve, emphasizing the importance of education, reskilling, and lifelong learning.

Additionally, as algorithms increasingly influence societal decisions, transparency and accountability become paramount. Ensuring that machine learning applications are ethical, unbiased, and inclusive remains a pressing challenge and a clarion call for responsible stewardship.

Conclusion: A Symphony of Innovation

Ultimately, the real-world applications of machine learning exemplify a symphony of innovation—one where data, algorithms, and human endeavor harmonize to create solutions that address both ancient and modern concerns. As machine learning continues to shape our world, it invites us to actively participate in the narrative it writes, ensuring that its deployment serves to uplift humanity, conserve our planet, and enrich our shared future.

4.5 Challenges and Limitations

Machine learning, often heralded as a digital savior, also harbors a Pandora's box of challenges and limitations. While the technologies may seem like mystical oracles of modern life, promising solutions to problems once thought insurmountable, they are not without their quirks and conundrums. As with any tool of great power, the elegance of machine learning is shadowed by potential pitfalls. Understanding these challenges is crucial for deploying these technologies responsibly and effectively.

The Data Dilemma: Quantity Meets Quality

The first hurdle in machine learning is akin to an age-old philosophical question: more precisely, the pursuit of quality versus quantity. While machine learning algorithms can process vast amounts of data, their performance is intrinsically tied to the quality and relevance of the data provided. Feeding them inadequate or biased data is much like expecting a chef to create a gourmet meal with spoiled ingredients.

Data collection often involves aggregating information from disparate sources, each with its own range of inaccuracies and inconsistencies. This variability can lead to the "garbage in, garbage out" phenomenon, where flawed data results in flawed predictions. Machine learning models, like impressionable students, absorb biases present in their training data, perpetuating and even amplifying these biases in their outputs. This has far-reaching implications, particularly when applied in sensitive areas such as hiring, law enforcement, and lending, where biased algorithms could propagate societal inequalities.

Moreover, large volumes of clean, high-quality data aren't always readily available—especially in nascent or highly specialized fields. In such cases, the scarcity of relevant data limits the feasibility of training robust and accurate models.

The Black Box Problem: Opacity and Interpretability

A second significant challenge is the "black box" nature of many machine learning models, particularly deep learning networks. While these models are adept at identifying patterns and making predictions, they often do so with an opacity that puzzles even the designers themselves. Consider asking a world-class chef to recreate a dish made by a rival without being able to watch the preparation or access the recipe—a daunting task indeed.

This lack of transparency poses severe issues, especially in sectors where accountability is paramount, like health-care or finance. Without clear understanding, it becomes difficult to diagnose why a model has made a particular decision or prediction. When a machine denies a bank loan application or misdiagnoses a medical condition, the inability to glean insight into the decision-making process can undermine trust and complicate regulatory compliance.

This opacity, known as the interpretability problem, demands solutions that illuminate the inner workings of complex models without sacrificing predictive accuracy. Efforts are underway to develop interpretable AI, using techniques that highlight which inputs are most influential in driving predictions, akin to providing clues to unlock the mysteries within the black box.

Computational Complexity: The Resource Conundrum

Learning from data is computationally expensive, particularly when training large, intricate models such as deep neural networks. These models require enormous amounts of processing power and time, necessitating specialized hardware like GPUs (Graphics Processing Units) and TPUs (Tensor Processing Units) to keep computational costs within reason.

The need for such resources presents barriers to entry for smaller organizations or individuals who lack the necessary infrastructure to train or utilize complex models. This barrier can exacerbate technological divides, limiting access to individuals or organizations that could otherwise benefit from machine learning advancements.

Moreover, the computational demands have an environmental impact. Data centers powering these processes consume substantial amounts of electricity, contributing to their carbon footprint. As machine learning applications become more widespread, reducing their environmental impact becomes a pressing concern. Green AI initiatives advocate for balancing the advancement of machine learning with carbon footprint minimization, exploring more efficient algorithms and renewable energy sources.

Ethics and Bias: The Human Element

As machine learning creep further into decision-making roles traditionally held by humans, ethical considerations take center stage. The rise of AI in societal systems brings forth dilemmas surrounding equity, justice, privacy, and consent.

Bias in machine learning is particularly pernicious, as

algorithms replicate the biases present in the data they are trained on. Historical prejudices and inequalities encoded into training data can manifest in machine learning outputs, perpetuating systemic discrimination. For example, facial recognition systems have been shown to perform inconsistently across different races or genders, which can have dire consequences if used inappropriately by law enforcement agencies.

Furthermore, there is the ever-present challenge of ensuring informed consent and data privacy. As algorithms parse personal data, concerns arise over whether individuals fully understand what information is being collected and how it is used. Data breaches and misuse have the potential to violate privacy rights, underscoring the need for stringent governance and transparent practices.

To tackle these challenges, interdisciplinary collaboration is essential, fostering a dialogue between ethicists, technologists, and policymakers. Building fairer, accountable systems involves auditing algorithms for bias, establishing ethical frameworks, and ensuring human oversight in decision-making processes.

Generalization versus Overfitting: The Balancing Act

Machine learning models face the dual challenges of generalization and overfitting—an intricate dance between being too simplistic and overly complex. A model is said to generalize well when it performs accurately not only on its training data but also on new, unseen data. Achieving this balance is akin to the sweet spot in a Goldilocks tale, where the porridge is neither too hot nor too cold.

Underfitting occurs when a model is too simple, failing to capture underlying patterns within the data. Overfitting, on the other hand, transpires when a model becomes too complex, memorizing the training data to the extent that it loses its ability to generalize. This paradox presents the need for comprehensive validation methods and processes, including feedback loops where model predictions are evaluated against real-world performance.

Regularization techniques, cross-validation, and data augmentation are tools employed in mitigating overfitting, emphasizing the iterative nature of model tuning and refinement.   Striking the right balance remains both an art and a science, inherently dependent upon the understanding and expertise of data scientists and engineers.

Legal and Regulatory Challenges: Navigating the Frameworks

Machine learning's permeation into diverse industries is outpacing the establishment of legal and regulatory frameworks designed to oversee its application safely and ethically.   Governments and policymakers face the daunting task of catching up with the rapid advancements and complexities machine learning introduces to sectors like healthcare, transport, and finance.

Concerns surrounding liability, accountability, and privacy necessitate the creation of innovative regulations that balance safety with innovation. The General Data Protection Regulation (GDPR) in Europe is an example of a legislative framework attempting to address some of these concerns, yet the international landscape remains fragmented, with practices and regulations varying significantly across regions.

Creating cohesive, adaptable frameworks for governance requires ongoing consultation and collaboration, establishing standards that preserve the benefits of machine learning while safeguarding public interest and trust.

Embracing and overcoming challenges

As the sphere of machine learning continues to evolve, so too will its challenges and limitations. Acknowledging these is not a declaration of defeat but an invitation to innovation—a call to address these challenges with creativity, collaboration, and conscience. Machine learning holds transformative potential but also demands vigilant stewardship. By navigating its complexities with humility, humanity can harness its capabilities to foster a future where technology and ethics coexist harmoniously, crafting solutions that honor both innovation and integrity.

Chapter 5

Deep Learning: The New Frontier

Deep learning represents a significant advancement in Artificial Intelligence, characterized by its ability to process vast amounts of data through multi-layered neural networks. This chapter explores the technological foundations that allow deep learning models, such as convolutional and recurrent neural networks, to perform complex tasks with remarkable accuracy. By examining the processes involved in training these models, it highlights both the breakthroughs and challenges associated with deep learning. The chapter further discusses the transformative applications of deep learning in fields such as computer vision and natural language processing, showcasing its potential and evolving impact.

5.1 The Rise of Deep Learning

Once confined to the realms of science fiction, artificial intelligence (AI) now inhabits our everyday lives, powered by the transformative force of deep learning. Unwrapping the story of this technological marvel reveals a tale of decades-long ingenuity, persistent challenges,

and finally, triumphant innovation driven by a confluence of factors such as increased computing power and
the explosion of accessible data.

Deep learning, at its heart, is inspired by the biological
learning processes of human brains. The key players in
this field are artificial neural networks, computational
constructs designed to mimic the intricate web of
neurons and synapses found in our gray matter. Yet,
the journey from simplistic neural networks to today's
sophisticated, multilayered architectures was neither
straightforward nor rapid.

In the early days, pioneers like Warren McCulloch and
Walter Pitts in the 1940s formulated the first conceptual
models of neural networks. Their work laid the foundation for the idea that, through networks of simple units,
complex computations could be simulated—an idea that
enthralled researchers with visions of machines capable
of mimicking human cognitive capabilities. However,
the initial surge of enthusiasm faced a fierce winter.

By the late 1950s, Frank Rosenblatt introduced the
perceptron, a linear model symbolizing an enthusiastic
hope for machine learning. Despite its initial promise in
solving simple classification problems, the perceptron's
limitations became apparent. The publication of the
book "Perceptrons" by Marvin Minsky and Seymour
Papert in 1969 had a chilling effect on neural network
research by demonstrating that single-layer perceptrons
could not solve non-linear problems like the XOR
problem. This led to the "AI Winter," a period of
reduced funding and interest in neural network
research.

Yet, like any good tale, this story of deep learning
features a resurgence. With renewed interest in the
mid-1980s, thanks to the introduction of the multi-layer

perceptron and the backpropagation algorithm, the field began to thaw. Researchers realized that layering neurons in multiple layers allowed for the solution of more complex tasks. This pivotal advancement was hindered, however, by the computational resources required to train such networks effectively.

Fast forward to the early 21st century, where a confluence of technological advancements ignited the deep learning revolution. The truly exponential increase in computing power—driven by the proliferation of GPUs tailored for parallel processing—provided the necessary horsepower to train extensively deep networks feasibly. Meanwhile, the digital age bore another gift: data, abundant and ripe for analysis, emerged from the collective digital activities of billions across the globe.

This abundance of data was crucial, for deep learning thrives on large quantities of data to function effectively. It was this data that enabled neural networks to learn the intricate patterns and subtleties needed to tackle complex problems, such as image and speech recognition, with unprecedented accuracy.

Moreover, as the world became more interconnected, frameworks and tools facilitating deep learning research became accessible to broader audiences. Platforms like TensorFlow and PyTorch removed the barriers to entry for burgeoning researchers and practitioners, democratizing the field and accelerating its growth at an astonishing pace.

Consider the realm of computer vision: once beleaguered by inaccuracies, it now stands as a testament to deep learning's power. With convolutional neural networks (CNNs), machines can identify and classify images with human-level precision, a feat once considered insurmountable. For example, AlexNet's groundbreaking success in the 2012 ImageNet competition demonstrated the practical superiority of deep networks over traditional computer vision methods.

Deep learning also revolutionized natural language processing (NLP). Models like recurrent neural networks (RNNs) and their sophisticated descendants, such as transformers, now excel at understanding and generating human language. These models power applications from real-time speech translation to content recommendation systems, seamlessly integrating into our daily digital experiences.

As we navigate the present technological landscape, deep learning's impact is omnipresent. In fields like healthcare, it aids in diagnostics by analyzing medical images with incredible precision.   In autonomous driving, it helps vehicles understand and navigate their environments safely.   The sheer scope of applications highlights deep learning's potential to reshape industries and redefine modern life.

Yet, the rise of deep learning brings with it a suite of challenges and ethical dilemmas. The appetite for vast datasets raises questions about privacy and data security. Furthermore, the opaqueness of deep models— their "black-box" nature—hinders interpretability, making it difficult to understand how decisions are made. As systems increasingly integrate into critical domains, these issues demand careful consideration and responsible stewardship.

The rise of deep learning represents a pivotal chapter in the annals of AI, marked by cycles of ambition and skepticism, ultimately culminating in transformative technology. This progression—from artificial neurons to algorithms emulating cortical functions—offers an inspiring testament to human ingenuity. As we further refine these systems and grapple with their implications, we stand on the cusp of an era where technological potential seems boundless, inviting us to dream boldly while remaining anchored in ethical and responsible innovation.

5.2 Neural Networks and Architectures

If deep learning were a concert, then neural networks would be its star performers—a dazzling ensemble composed of countless simple units working in harmony to produce a symphony of computation. These architectures are the beating heart of deep learning, transforming abstract concepts about machine intelligence into functional reality.

At a fundamental level, an artificial neural network (ANN) is an assembly of interconnected nodes, akin to neurons in the human brain. Each node, or "neuron," processes input signals, transforming them with a weighted sum, adding a bias, and passing the result through an activation function. This operation simulates the way biological neurons might fire or remain dormant, enabling the network to model complex decision boundaries.

The simplest form of neural network, known as the feed-forward neural network, operates in a single direction—input flows to output without looping back—similar to a well-rehearsed monologue. Data enters through input layers, journeys through hidden layers, and emerges transformed in the output layer. This structure, while elegant, serves as a foundation for the more intricate architectures that we shall explore.

To appreciate the exquisite variety of neural networks, one must begin with the multi-layer perceptron (MLP), the ancestor of modern architectures. The MLP introduced the revolutionary concept of multiple hidden layers, overcoming the limitations of single-layer models and allowing for the learning of non-linear mappings. However, MLPs rely heavily on data preprocessing and are not particularly efficient in dealing with structured data, such as images or sequences, where feature hierarchies are crucial.

Enter convolutional neural networks (CNNs), the maestros of computer vision. CNNs are designed to process grid-like data structures, most notably images, by imitating the visual cortex of animals. They employ convolutional layers, where a small filter slides across the input data, detecting patterns such as edges, textures, and more complex features layer by layer. This local connectivity drastically reduces the number of parameters and ensures translation invariance—a crucial property that allows CNNs to recognize objects in varying positions and contexts.

CNNs perform impressively well in tasks like image classification and object detection. Their prowess is perhaps best illustrated by their applications in self-driving cars, where they interpret visual data from cameras to identify road signs, pedestrians, and other vehicles, all while making split-second decisions.

While CNNs excel in spatial data, understanding sequences—a series of data points, where order matters—is better suited to a different kind of network. Recurrent neural networks (RNNs) come into play here with their ability to cycle through their input, maintaining "memory" of previous inputs. This architecture is akin to a storyteller recalling the plot's details to weave a narrative seamlessly.

RNNs are particularly valuable in language processing tasks, such as machine translation and sentiment analysis. However, they often grapple with two notorious challenges: vanishing and exploding gradients. Essentially, as RNNs process long sequences, the gradients used to update weights during training can diminish to insignificance or grow uncontrollably, impeding learning.

To counteract these issues, Long Short-Term Memory networks (LSTMs) and Gated Recurrent Units (GRUs) were developed. These variants introduce gating mechanisms to control the flow of information, ensuring that pertinent information is retained over extended sequences, akin to placing bookmarks within a lengthy novel to quickly retrieve important passages.

Another enticing architecture in the neural network symphony is the transformer, an innovation that has recently taken the AI world by storm, especially in natural language processing. Unlike RNNs, transformers do not rely on sequence order; instead, they employ mechanisms called attention to assess the importance of each part of the input data. This approach allows for parallel processing, dramatically speeding up the training and inference processes—much like harmonizing a choir where each voice is crucial but independently assessed for its contribution to the overall melody.

The transformer model has led to groundbreaking developments in language models, with applications ranging from chatbots to large-scale language generation systems, exemplars of which are OpenAI's GPT models. These systems delve deep into vast corpora of text

111

to generate human-like responses, elevating NLP to unprecedented heights.

As we wade deeper into the ocean of neural network architectures, we encounter the compelling field of generative models. Here, networks such as Generative Adversarial Networks (GANs) and Variational Autoencoders (VAEs) take center stage, not only predicting or classifying data but also creating new data instances. GANs play a thrilling game of cat and mouse, with two networks—the generator and discriminator—pitted against each other to produce increasingly realistic data outputs. Artists and designers leverage GANs to create stunning visual art, generate realistic voices, or even design products, blurring the lines between reality and simulation.

Despite the reach and creativity offered by these myriad architectures, neural networks are not without challenges. They often require enormous amounts of data and computational power, which can be prohibitive. Moreover, the "black-box" nature of these models raises questions of transparency and trust—how decisions are reached may remain obscured. Engineers and scientists are actively working on strategies to make these models more interpretable—a critical pursuit as we increasingly integrate AI into essential systems that demand accountability.

In exploring the vast landscape of neural network architectures, we find ourselves in a realm where human ingenuity meets technological alchemy. These networks turn the abstract notion of machine intelligence into tangible outcomes, continuously expanding our capabilities to understand and transform the world. As these architectures evolve, each contributes uniquely to the rich tapestry of deep learning, propelling us into a future where the boundaries of possibility are ever extended and redefined.

5.3   Training Deep Models

Imagine attempting to teach an untrained chef to cook a gourmet meal. You'd likely start with a recipe, guiding them through each step, tweaking their approach until the desired taste is achieved. Training deep models follows a similar pedagogical journey, rooted in iteration, correction, and refinement. In this high-stakes culinary adventure of artificial intelligence, the sous-chef is data, and the recipe is backpropagation—flavored with a dash of gradient descent.

Training deep models is akin to unlocking their potential, enabling them to see, hear, speak, and act. At its core, training is about adjusting the numerous parameters— often millions—that govern how these models transform inputs into outputs. The magic ingredient? Optimization, the sophisticated art of helping a model improve upon its tasks by providing clear feedback and direction.

But how exactly do these models learn? Let's take a walk through the process, starting with the data—the lifeblood of deep learning. Consider it as a rich tapestry of experiences, stories, and facts upon which a model reflects and draws insights. From vast image libraries like ImageNet to the seemingly endless text of the World Wide Web, data provides direction to models, teaching them to detect patterns and make informed decisions.

As with our culinary example, the training process demands a goal, or more precisely, a loss function that quantifies the model's errors. Imagine a loss function as a discerning culinary critic whose palate is never appeased until perfection is achieved. It measures the divergence between the model's predictions and

113

the actual expected outcomes. In response, the model adjusts its internal parameters to improve its "culinary creations," so to speak.

But adjustment is where things get intriguing. Enter the elegant mechanism of backpropagation, the process by which neural networks update their weights. When an error is detected, backpropagation works backward through the network, akin to a meticulous chef tracing back through each misstep in the preparation to rectify a dish. By computing the gradient of the loss function relative to each weight, it identifies the direction in which adjustments should be made—preferably with just enough force to enhance the recipe without overwhipping the meringue.

The technique that translates these adjustments into practice is gradient descent. Picture it as a hiker descending a mountainous loss landscape, each step attempting to find the lowest point, or global minimum, where the model's performance is optimal. Various flavors of gradient descent exist—some stride boldly, while others tiptoe with caution, depending on the needs of the model and the terrain.

The simplest version, known as batch gradient descent, computes the gradient using the entire dataset. Imagine the hiker pausing, studying every rock and tree, before taking a step. It can be slow but precise. Conversely, stochastic gradient descent (SGD) takes impromptu steps, using only one data point at a time, much like a hiker darting down the hill in a series of spontaneous leaps—an approach that's surprisingly efficient for deep models. Mini-batch gradient descent offers a compromise, using a handful of samples, balancing between stability and speed.

Tuning the learning rate—the stride length of our

hiker—is crucial for effective descent. Too long, and the hiker may overshoot into perilous heights; too short, and progress dribbles to a halt. Clever adjustments and adaptive learning rates, like those seen in the Adam optimizer, help models dance gracefully across the landscape, adjusting learning rates on the fly to suit varied terrains, akin to a dancer responding dynamically to music's tempo.

Naturally, no hike is without its unseen challenges. The spectral presence of overfitting looms large—a trap where models memorize the training data with precision, yet fail spectacularly when faced with new data, akin to a chef who perfects a single dish but falters with anything new. Addressing overfitting involves tactics like regularization, reducing the model's complexity, dropout techniques (randomly ignoring certain neurons during training to encourage diversity), or employing data augmentation—enhancing the training set by introducing variations that reflect real-world situations.

Another obstacle hinders the journey—vanishing and exploding gradients. These phenomena are akin to losing one's bearings on a fog-shrouded cliffside or being overwhelmed by cascading boulders. Vanishing gradients make it difficult to discern where to step next, as the signals become too faint to detect, particularly in deeper networks. Techniques such as normalization strategies—batch normalization or layer normalization— act as guideposts, helping steer the optimization process through treacherous paths.

It's also pertinent to navigate the ethical and philosophical terrain of selecting and curating data. Imbalances and biases ingrained within training datasets can propagate through the models, leading to unintended consequences or unfair decisions, much like a chef who, unknowingly, relies on spoiled ingredients. Awareness, transparency, and continual evaluation are vital in ensuring the culinary delights created by deep models are palatable and beneficial to all.

Despite these challenges, training deep models has democratized expertise, enabling machines to master image recognition, articulate thoughts, and even diagnose diseases.   Consider AlphaGo, the neural network paradigm that bested human champions in the complex game of Go—a testament not just to the power of deep models, but to thoughtful, iterative training.

Each model, once naïve, undergoes a metamorphosis through the alchemical process of training.   Like a master chef refining each dish, these models learn to analyze, understand, and generate, driven by feedback, structured optimization, and relentless pursuit toward perfection.   As we reach the peaks of accomplishment and glimpse the expansive possibilities below, the path of training deep models continues to invite exploration, innovation, and, perhaps most importantly, a continued commitment to ethical development.

In this remarkable intersection of technology and human creativity, training deep models leads not only to more capable machines but to deeper questions about intelligence, learning, and the essence of understanding itself. The journey is only beginning, inviting us to ponder not just what machines can achieve, but how they learn, adapt, and, perchance, transform the world we live in.

5.4   Applications of Deep Learning

Deep learning has become the virtuoso of our digital age, deftly touching almost every field with its transformative potential.   From autonomous vehicles to personal voice assistants, the applications of deep learning have shifted from far-off dreams to integral components of our daily routines, reshaping industries and societal norms along the way.

Begin with the world of vision—computer vision, to be precise—where machines are no longer blind followers of predefined logic but keen observers capable of interpreting the visual world with unprecedented precision. Convolutional neural networks (CNNs), the maestros of this domain, have enabled applications that see and understand beyond raw pixels.

Consider autonomous vehicles: once an avant-garde concept, these self-driving wonders rely heavily on deep learning to navigate complex and dynamic environments. Through a symphony of sensors and cameras, combined with robust vision algorithms, such vehicles can detect obstacles, read traffic signs, and anticipate the movements of pedestrians and other vehicles—a task requiring almost human-like comprehension. Companies like Tesla and Waymo are at the forefront, constantly refining their models to ensure safety and efficiency.

In the field of healthcare, deep learning is imparting a diagnostic acuity akin to seasoned medical practitioners. Medical imaging, including MRI and CT scans, is interpreted by neural networks that can identify anomalies with accuracy often surpassing human experts. Consider the early detection of diseases such as diabetic retinopathy, where models analyze retinal scans with adept success, significantly improving patient outcomes through early intervention.

Stepping into the realm of sound, deep learning powers advancements in speech recognition, enabling a more natural interaction between humans and machines.

117

From Apple's Siri to Amazon's Alexa, voice-activated assistants have become conversational partners in our homes, offices, and even cars. Recurrent neural networks (RNNs) and transformers parse our spoken language, transforming it into actionable commands or insightful responses, paving the way for seamless human-machine symbiosis.

Deep learning's prowess stretches further into the domain of natural language processing (NLP). Here, machines not only understand but also generate human language, facilitating translations, sentiment analysis, and even creative writing. Language models—such as OpenAI's GPT-3—demonstrate the capability to produce text that is often indistinguishable from that penned by humans, revolutionizing content creation, customer service, and educational tools.

In fraud detection and cybersecurity, deep learning's ability to learn patterns and anomalies proves invaluable. Financial institutions deploy neural networks to spot suspicious activities with efficacy beyond traditional methods. These models continuously learn from transaction data, updating their parameters to distinguish between benign and fraudulent activities swiftly—akin to having a security expert constantly on patrol.

E-commerce has equally embraced deep learning as a catalyst for enhanced customer experiences. Recommendation systems, powered by neural networks, curate personalized shopping experiences by analyzing user behavior, preferences, and purchase history. Amazon's recommendation engine, a staple of modern digital commerce, exemplifies how deep learning personalizes and anticipates consumer desires to an uncanny degree.

The arts and entertainment industries haven't escaped the transformative touch of deep learning. From creating new music compositions to generating visual art, generative models like Generative Adversarial Networks (GANs) offer novel forms of artistic expression. Musicians and artists collaborate with models to explore innovative soundscapes and visuals, challenging traditional notions of creativity and authorship.

Even in agriculture, deep learning emerges as a revolutionary force. Precision agriculture leverages aerial images analyzed by neural networks to assess crop health, predict yields, and identify pest infestations. Farmers employ these insights to make data-driven decisions, optimizing resource usage and increasing productivity in sustainable ways.

Despite its expansive reach, the implementation of deep learning applications surfaces ethical and practical challenges. The privacy concerns associated with data collection must be meticulously managed to prevent misuse. Moreover, the potential for biases within models—reflecting the biases present in their training data—demands vigilant oversight to ensure fairness and equity.

The ecological cost of training deep models also necessitates scrutiny. The computational resources required can be immense, prompting research into more energy-efficient architectures and training methods, ensuring that technological advancements align with environmental sustainability goals.

Reflecting on the transformative power of deep learning applications, one cannot help but ponder the broader implications. As these technologies continue to advance, they redefine not just industries, but the very fabric of our daily lives. They invite a philosophical discourse on the nature of intelligence, creativity, and the interplay between humans and machines in an increasingly automated world.

Deep learning's myriad applications usher us into an era of remarkable possibilities, where machines not only assist but augment human potential. As we witness this technological symphony unfold, our task remains to harness these advancements wisely, steering towards a future where technology serves as a force for good, enhancing the human experience in profound and lasting ways.

5.5 Challenges in Deep Learning

Deep learning, often lauded for its formidable prowess, is not without its tribulations. Enthralled by its successes, we must not overlook the formidable challenges that accompany this technological marvel. These obstacles, far from insurmountable, demand our attention and ingenuity, like intricate puzzles awaiting ingenious solutions.

Consider first the enigma of data dependency. Deep learning's insatiable hunger for data requires vast amounts of information to learn meaningful patterns. While we revel in an era of data abundance, not all datasets are created equal. Quality, diversity, and representativeness remain paramount, as models trained on skewed or biased datasets often inherit these imperfections, leading to erroneous or unfair outcomes. For instance, inadequate representation of minority groups in training data can result in models that perform poorly across diverse demographics—a critical concern in applications such as facial recognition or loan approval systems.

This data dependency tango leads us to privacy and ethical dilemmas. The collection and utilization of sensitive personal data must balance the dual demands of progress and privacy. Striking this balance is akin to walking a tightrope, where missteps can have significant consequences, from data breaches to the erosion of public trust. Legislative frameworks like the GDPR in Europe have emerged to guide responsible data handling, yet questions of data ownership and consent persist in our digitally interconnected world.

Moving on, the notorious "black-box" nature of deep learning models poses a riddle of interpretability. Much like admiring a well-executed magic trick without understanding its workings, deep models can produce remarkably accurate predictions while obscuring the logic behind them. This opacity can be problematic, particularly in high-stakes domains like healthcare or finance, where understanding the reasoning behind decisions is crucial for trust and accountability.

Efforts to demystify these opaque boxes have spawned a new branch of research focused on explainable AI (XAI). Techniques vary from visualizing neuron activations to developing interpretable surrogate models that approximate the behavior of their inscrutable counterparts. The ideal is to transform these black boxes into something resembling a "glass box," where decisions are not only comprehensible but justifiable.

As we delve deeper, we encounter the scientific conundrum of overfitting. This phenomenon occurs when a model becomes an overzealous student, memorizing training data to perfection but floundering when presented with new situations. The challenge lies in teaching the model to generalize, akin to imparting creative problem-solving skills rather than rote memorization. Techniques such as regularization, dropout, and data augmentation endeavor to cultivate this resilience, helping models perform robustly outside the confines of their training data.

Training deep models also incurs significant computational costs. The formidable power required to learn from immense datasets, epitomized by models like GPT-3, presents not just an economic burden but an environmental one. Concerns about energy consumption and carbon footprints necessitate a reassessment of how we develop and deploy these technologies. Research is pivoting towards more efficient architectures, spurred by the growing imperative to harmonize advancement with sustainability.

As deep learning models grow, so too does their susceptibility to adversarial attacks—a game of cat and mouse where tiny, often imperceptible perturbations in input data can dramatically skew outputs. Illustrations of this vulnerability are unsettling: imperceptible noise added to images can cause a state-of-the-art classifier to mistake a panda for a gibbon. This fragility poses serious security concerns, particularly in applications like autonomous vehicles or medical diagnostics, where adversarially altered inputs could have dire consequences.

To counter these threats, researchers are developing strategies that bolster the robustness of deep models. Techniques range from enhancing training data with adversarial examples to more advanced defenses like robust optimization. Yet, this remains an arms race, with new attack vectors emerging as quickly as the defenses against them, underscoring the need for continuous vigilance.

Finally, the ethical landscape of deep learning cannot be ignored. The deployment of AI systems wields profound societal impact, necessitating a focus on the responsible and fair development of these technologies. Issues of bias, accountability, and transparency loom large over deep learning applications, compelling developers and stakeholders to wrestle with profound ethical questions: Who is accountable when AI fails? How do we ensure that systems align with human values?

Initiatives like AI Ethics boards and inclusive design processes are steps toward addressing these dilemmas, fostering discussions that prioritize inclusivity and fairness. Nonetheless, the rapid pace of AI advancement often outstrips the development of cohesive regulatory frameworks, compelling us to reflect on the broader impact of technology on humanity.

Amidst these challenges, the narrative of deep learning remains one of promise and exploration. While the hurdles are formidable, they present opportunities for innovation and growth. As we grapple with these issues, collaboration across disciplines, from computer science and engineering to law and philosophy, is imperative.

In confronting and overcoming these challenges, we pave the way for a future where deep learning not only pushes the boundaries of what's possible but does so in a manner that is equitable, sustainable, and transparent. The journey ahead invites us to embrace this dual mission—pioneering technological wonder with a mindful eye on ethical stewardship—ensuring that the benefits of deep learning serve the greater good.

Chapter 6

Natural Language Processing

Natural Language Processing (NLP) is a vital area of Artificial Intelligence focusing on the interaction between humans and computers through language. This chapter provides a detailed examination of the core components of NLP, including tokenization, parsing, and semantic analysis, which are essential for understanding and processing language. It discusses popular techniques like sentiment analysis and machine translation, illustrating their application in real-world scenarios such as chatbots and voice assistants. Additionally, the chapter addresses the challenges of contextual understanding and ambiguity, highlighting the complexities involved in achieving effective language processing across different cultures and languages.

6.1 Understanding Natural Language Processing

Imagine speaking to your smartphone and having it flawlessly interpret your intricate request, answer your query, or even engage you in a chat about the weather. All this magic, often taken for granted, is brought to life

by the field of Natural Language Processing (NLP)—
a fascinating domain within Artificial Intelligence
(AI) that bridges human language with machine
understanding. But how does NLP endow computers
with the seeming ability to comprehend language, a feat
once thought the sole preserve of human intelligence?

At its core, NLP attempts to unravel the mysteries
of human language, empowering machines to parse,
interpret, and generate it with fidelity. The essence of
NLP is not merely about having machines understand
words, but grasping the context, nuances, and subtleties
that render human communication astonishingly rich.
This pursuit nestles itself within the broader aim of AI
to emulate human-like understanding and interaction.

To appreciate the full spectrum of NLP, it's beneficial to
embark on a brief historical journey. The roots of NLP
stretch back to the mid-20th century, entwined with the
genesis of computer science and linguistics. Alan Turing,
often celebrated as the father of computer science, specu-
lated early on about machines imitating human conversation. His 1950 paper posed a pivotal question, "Can
machines think?"—essentially laying the philosophical
groundwork for future language-processing endeavors.

By the 1950s, computational linguistics began to emerge
as a promising field, with early experiments in machine
translation offering glimpses of the potential held by
computers for language tasks. These pioneering efforts,
however, were encumbered by naive assumptions about
the ease of automating language understanding. Indeed,
initial translations, such as those between Russian and
English during the Cold War, often resulted in comical
inaccuracies, underscoring the complexity of language.

Advancements in computational power, theoretical
linguistics, and algorithm development continued

to nourish NLP's gradual evolution. The 1970s and 1980s witnessed the rise of rule-based systems, where painstakingly crafted grammatical rules informed the parsing and interpretation of text. Yet, the brittleness of such systems—unable to adapt to language's inherent variability—soon became apparent.

It wasn't until the late 20th century, with the advent of machine learning, that NLP began to metamorphose into its current, more agile form. Machine learning offered a departure from hand-crafted rules, leveraging statistical patterns in large datasets to enable flexible and adaptive language models. These models could glean insights from text corpora, facilitating more robust and sophisticated language understanding.

Consider, for example, the task of language translation— the very challenge that initially exposed the naivety of early NLP approaches. Today's translation systems, powered by neural networks and vast multilingual datasets, deliver remarkably accurate results, translating idiomatic expressions and context with surprising precision.   Such sophistication owes much to the burgeoning realms of deep learning and the trifecta of data, algorithms, and computational power that fuel contemporary NLP.

However, appreciating NLP's accomplishments necessitates recognizing its components and processes. To imbibe a machine with linguistic acumen, several layers of analysis occur. These start with **tokenization**, where raw text divides into manageable pieces like words and sentences. Each unit then undergoes **parsing**, a critical juncture where the system dissects grammatical structures to understand the relationships between words.

Moving deeper, **semantic analysis** tackles meaning by discerning the intent behind phrases and sentences.

Here, context becomes king. Words like "bank" pose challenges, bearing multiple meanings ranging from financial institutions to river edges—distinctions clear to humans but historically elusive for machines. NLP systems must grapple with these variabilities, often exuding elegance in their ability to infer correct meanings through contextual clues.

Another critical facet of NLP lies in **pragmatics**, the study of how context influences interpretation, varying in scope from immediate conversational context to broader sociocultural factors. This layer adds more complexity to the NLP stack, demanding a nuanced consideration of language that transcends simple word conceptions.

Of note is the rise of contemporary applications hinging on NLP prowess. Beyond the everyday convenience of chatbots handling customer queries, consider voice-activated virtual assistants like Alexa or Siri. These assistants marshal the full might of NLP, transforming spoken language into actionable commands, all while accommodating diverse accents and linguistic idiosyncrasies. Another practical application is in sentiment analysis, where NLP algorithms parse social media, reviews, or feedback to gauge public opinion, influencing everything from marketing strategies to political campaigns.

Yet, even with these profound achievements, NLP grapples with persistent challenges. Language's inherently idiosyncratic nature, with its idioms, metaphors, and cultural dependencies, remains a daunting labyrinth for NLP systems to navigate. The endeavor to achieve contextual understanding, where context is woven into every facet of interpretation, signifies a frontier still being explored. Here, larger language models, such as OpenAI's GPT series, showcase incremental advances, generating text that mirrors human-like qualities in structure and creativity, pushing the boundaries of what NLP might achieve.

Furthermore, as NLP grows in sophistication, it beckons ethical considerations. From biases embedded in training data spilling into machine behavior to privacy concerns arising from data-driven technologies, these issues necessitate careful oversight and conscientious design.

In summary, the story of Natural Language Processing is one of remarkable ingenuity and incessant pursuit of linguistic harmony between man and machine. From fumbling translations of yesteryears to the elegant parsing of today, NLP underscores technological evolution's potential to bridge the chasm between human expression and computational comprehension. As it continues to evolve, NLP not only deepens our interaction with technology but also perpetually challenges our understanding of language itself, offering a rich tapestry for future explorations.

6.2 Core Components of NLP

The endeavor to endow machines with an understanding of human language might seem akin to teaching a rock to dance—not an entirely impossible task, but one requiring careful choreography. At the heart of this grand endeavor lie the core components of Natural Language Processing (NLP), the building blocks that break down the abstract art of human communication into digital processes a machine can parse, analyze, and respond to. Unraveling the fabric of language into these components illuminates the intricate dance steps that transform cold calculus into warm conversational magic.

Let's commence with perhaps the most intuitive process:

129

tokenization, where the vast continuum of human text transforms into discrete units—tokens—that serve as NLP's fundamental particles. Picture a sentence akin to an elegant pearl necklace; tokenization is the act of gently unclasping it, laying each pearl bare. By splitting a text into distinct words or phrases, tokenization establishes a foundation upon which further analysis can build. This process extends beyond simple word separation, adapting to challenges like recognizing contractions, hyphenated words, and ensuring punctuation doesn't steal the show as independent tokens.

Following tokenization, text is ripe for *morphological analysis*, where the intricate dressing of words—their prefixes, suffixes, roots, and spelling variants—is analyzed. Consider the word "running," which morphologically splits into the root "run" and the suffix "ing." Understanding these morphological nuances allows systems to group and interpret words that share the same base meaning, regardless of tense or context variations.

Once the language is stripped to its core elements, the task of *syntactic parsing* begins. Syntactic parsing likens to casting the actors of a play and assigning them roles, identifying the subject, the verb, and the object within a sentence. It's where grammatical structure is scrutinized and sentences are deconstructed according to linguistic hierarchies. Historically, this component took cues from traditional grammar studies, though it now often leverages statistical or machine-learned models to account for language's unpredictability.

Driven by syntactic parsing's informative insights, *semantic analysis* delves into meaning.   It's akin to interpreting a director's vision—the substance behind each line of dialogue, seeking out not just phrases, but resonating truths.   Here, meanings of words and the clauses in which they reside are analyzed with respect

130

to context, exposing the intended message beyond mere wordplay. This process contemplates polysemy (where a word has multiple meanings), synonyms (different words sharing a similar meaning), and word sense disambiguation—ensuring that "bank" is recognized as either a place to safeguard cash or a scenic riverside.

Alongside semantic analysis lies *pragmatic analysis*, which hones in on what is often left unsaid amid words. Language, after all, doesn't exist in a vacuum; it flows with cultural undercurrents and social contexts. Pragmatics contemplates who is speaking, to whom, where, and why. It grapples with what might seem trivial—intonations, pauses, and implications—yet is crucial for authentic communication. For machines, capturing these subtleties paves the way to richer and more accurate language interactions.

Beyond analysis of singular statements, the broader battle for comprehension extends to *discourse integration*. This holistic step considers a sequence of statements, threading the narrative to maintain context and coherence. Ensuring that ensuing sentences logically connect allows machines to comprehend storylines, instructions, or any complex body of text. Here, anaphora resolution—the method to decipher phrases like "he," "she," or "it" in reference to previously mentioned entities—plays a pivotal role.

Sitting at the intersection of these components is the emotionally driven process of *sentiment analysis*. Understandably veering into the territory of applied NLP rather than pure componentry, sentiment analysis is nonetheless essential. It mines text not merely for information but for emotional tone—a sentiment which steers brand strategies, shapes political discourse, and more.

Each component of NLP harmonizes within a greater

131

framework—much like sections of an orchestra syncing to create a symphony. While individually potent, their potency exponentially increases when in concert, delivering tools capable of parsing resumes, translating texts, powering chatbots, and auto-completing emails. Uniting statistics with linguistics, these interwoven stages highlight the delicate balancing act of addressing language's surface form and its implicit substance.

Consider the real-world implications: when you ask a virtual assistant to "set a timer for twenty minutes," the command isn't merely recognized by rote. NLP burrows through layers—tokenizing the request, parsing commands, extracting meaning, and applying contextual pragmatics to correctly execute the task. Whether the request was issued vocally, typed, or even inferred, each component plays a crucial role in ensuring the machine accurately deciphers the person's intention.

This seamless back-and-forth wouldn't be possible in NLP's infancy during the mid-20th century. Yet, technological evolution, expanding data sources, and novel algorithms have carved a space where machines increasingly comprehend our commands, satiating the cognitive appetites of humans with responses and actions that begin to ape true understanding.

Despite tremendous advances, NLP remains an impermanent masterpiece—constantly evolving and striving to address ever-present limitations. Ambiguities in language, cultural context variations, and nuanced emotional undertones challenge even the most adept systems. But as machines continue learning in our linguistically rich sandbox, the nuanced harmony of core NLP components fuels an ongoing dialogue between human creativity and machine interpretation.

Through these components, NLP emerges not just as a technical ambition, but as a mirror reflecting our desire to connect with the technology we create—an invitation to explore language as an interface not only to machines but a deeper understanding of ourselves. Undoubtedly, as these components mature and redefine possibilities, the future will hold even richer seams of interaction, forever blurring the line between human and machine linguistics.

6.3 Popular NLP Techniques

Picture yourself strolling through a library where the books talk back, or imagine a friend who can fluently converse in any language you choose. These playful visions, while fanciful, are emblematic of the very real advancements and applications born from Popular Natural Language Processing (NLP) Techniques. As we delve into this vibrant realm, we'll explore the techniques that fuel everything from insightful sentiment analysis to the astoundingly nuanced translations that characterize modern linguistic technology. Let us embark on this journey through the prism of both historical context and contemporary innovation, shedding light on how NLP continues to shape and reflect our aspirations.

One cornerstone technique that has captured both scholarly and commercial imagination is **sentiment analysis**. Often likened to having machines act as emotional barometers, sentiment analysis involves deciphering the emotional tone behind textual data—a tool greatly cherished by marketers and political pundits alike. This technique analyzes language to determine whether the sentiment expressed is positive, negative, or neutral, effectively transforming strings of text into indicators of mood or opinion.

Initially, sentiment analysis appeared on the scene as a blunt instrument, limited to counting positive or negative words. Yet, the sophistication has grown exponentially. Now, it often involves using machine learning algorithms that recognize patterns in text, allowing for more nuanced interpretations. Imagine a Twitter feed buzzing with news of a celebrity's latest venture. Sentiment analysis can swiftly distill thousands of tweets, offering companies valuable insights into public opinion in a flash—a clear example of its profound impact on real-world decision-making.

Next, we venture into **machine translation**, arguably one of NLP's most celebrated feats and a technique steeped in storied history. In its early phases, pioneers dreamt boldly of automatic translation systems capable of bridging any linguistic divide. Those efforts, while groundbreaking, often generated humorously inaccurate translations. Fast forward to today, and we find ourselves in an era where machine translation engines, such as Google Translate, routinely convert text and speech across numerous languages with impressive fluency.

The power of modern machine translation arises from advanced models like neural networks, particularly neural machine translation (NMT), which leverages deep learning to improve accuracy by considering entire sentences as context rather than word-by-word translation. This leap forward allows systems to better capture nuances, idioms, and syntactic peculiarities. Use it while traveling in a foreign country, and you might see once-daunting language barriers transform into mere linguistic hurdles.

Strolling further down this neurological path, we

encounter **text summary generation**—a testament to the age-old adage "Brevity is the soul of wit." Text summarization condenses large volumes of content into digestible summaries, a necessity in our current age of information overload. Two primary approaches are prevalent: extractive, which isolates and compiles key sentences from the original text, and abstractive, which reworks ideas to encapsulate the essence, akin to how a human might summarize an article.

Imagine being a journalist needing quick insights or a scholarly researcher sifting through piles of academic papers. An effective text summarization algorithm can save time and prioritize the key takeaways, converting daunting text bodies into succinct knowledge bites.

The subtly complex art of **named entity recognition** (**NER**) follows. This technique involves identifying and categorizing distinct entities within a text, such as names of people, organizations, locations, and dates. You're likely already benefiting from NER if you've noticed how swiftly your email can identify an event date and suggest adding it to your calendar.

NER's roots might seem mechanical at first glance—akin to an electronic phonebook of sorts—but dig deeper, and its applications prove diverse and critical. Picture a legal context, where extracting case-specific data from dense legal documents can streamline processes drastically. NER serves as a crucial filtration tool, isolating the who, where, and when amid the sea of data.

As we further probe the landscape of popular NLP techniques, let's not overlook **speech recognition**—the magic behind your experience with virtual assistants like Siri or Alexa. Speech recognition techniques convert spoken language into text, a process whose accuracy has

135

skyrocketed due to advances in acoustic modeling and the deployment of recurrent neural networks (RNNs). These systems are trained on extensive data sets that represent a vast range of accents and speech patterns, creating a depth of understanding unimaginable even a decade ago.

Finally, consider **topic modeling**, a technique that serves as a thematic tour guide through any collection of texts. Topic modeling algorithms, like Latent Dirichlet Allocation (LDA), uncover patterns that represent topics within text corpora. This capability is invaluable for organizations needing to discern trends in customer feedback or for academics conducting text analysis in social sciences.

Despite its seemingly esoteric nature, topic modeling strikes a chord in practical realms. Consider a company longing to understand emerging trends reflected in customer reviews—or an academic who wants to decode themes in a century's worth of literary works. These models uncover the latent themes, rendering torrents of unstructured data into structured insights.

Reflecting on the richness and variety of these popular NLP techniques, it's inspiring to consider how they impact daily life, often quietly, enhancing productivity, understanding, and connectivity. Sentiment analysis shapes brand strategies, machine translation bridges cultures, and speech recognition augments accessibility, symbolizing merely a fraction of possibilities.

As we continue developing these techniques within the ever-changing tapestry of human language, questions persist regarding their ethical implications and inherent biases. Understanding and mitigating these biases offer a horizon of challenges, reminding us of language's role as not just a tool for communication but a vessel of cultural identity and personal expression.

In essence, these popular NLP techniques continue to enrich our interaction with the digital world, drawing us ever closer to our machines in a dialogue laced with both potential and complexity. Each application serves as a stepping stone, illuminating paths forward in our quest to grasp the nuances of human language and elevate our digital interaction in ever more profound and personalized ways.

6.4 NLP Applications and Tools

Natural Language Processing (NLP) isn't just an academic fascination; it's a dynamic force transforming the digital landscape, infiltrating our lives in myriad ways we often overlook. From the saccharine politeness of a virtual assistant to the finely tuned marketing campaigns that seem to read our minds, the applications of NLP are as varied as they are profound. In this exploration, we dive deep into the cornucopia of NLP applications and tools, illuminating both their history and their indispensable role in today's increasingly interconnected world.

First, let us stroll through the familiar terrain of **chatbots and virtual assistants**, where Siri, Alexa, and the like have blazed a populist trail. These tools exemplify NLP's triumph in blending conversational fluency with technological function. Chatbots and virtual assistants serve as bridges between human intent and machine execution, parsing our often convoluted requests with delightful aplomb. Powered by NLP, they don't just parse words, but interpret intent, drawing from vast datasets to understand queries that may have the elegance of poetry or the complexity of legalese.

137

The charm of such technology rests in its accessibility and adaptability. From setting alarms and controlling smart homes to providing weather forecasts or even conversational companionship, the utility of virtual assistants cannot be overstated. Imagine a company seeking to streamline customer service operations; an NLP-fueled chatbot can handle routine inquiries while freeing human representatives to tackle more nuanced concerns, optimizing resources and customer experience alike.

Language translation tools mark another arena dramatically reshaped by NLP. The evolution from elementary translation programs into complex systems like Google Translate reflects decades of research and innovation. Today, these tools offer far more than rudimentary word swaps—they recognize context, idioms, and conversational subtleties, rendering them indispensable for global communication. Businesses harness translation tools to breach linguistic boundaries, thereby opening new markets and fostering global collaboration.

Moreover, the influence of NLP extends into realms of **content and document management**, significantly altering how information is curated and accessed. Tools powered by NLP perform text categorization, summarization, and indexing autonomously. Libraries, media houses, and corporations leverage these capabilities to sift through troves of documents efficiently, ensuring swift retrieval of pertinent information and the distillation of knowledge from vast datasets.

Consider the pressurized environment of a newsroom where time is perpetually of the essence. An NLP application can analyze large volumes of textual data, summarize it into gleaming shards of information, and even suggest themes and topics that might escape the hurried human eye. These capabilities are realized through sophisticated NLP methodologies, which discern patterns and contextually relevant insights, thereby transforming raw data into pivotal stories faster than ever.

A platform that often benefits from NLP's prowess is social media, a volatile cauldron of public opinion and trends. Here, **sentiment analysis** plays a crucial role in gauging the emotional tone of posts on platforms like Twitter and Facebook. Companies wield this insight to tailor marketing strategies, politicians to recalibrate messages, and analysts to anticipate stock movements. It's akin to giving brands a pair of ears to the digital ether, allowing them to listen even to the whispers of discontent or jubilation, adjusting their strategies nimbly in response.

NLP tools are also carving niches in fields like **healthcare**. Consider a future where comprehensive patient histories, symptoms, and research papers form a cohesive resource accessible via an NLP interface. Hospitals and healthcare providers are already experimenting with such interfaces to facilitate better diagnostic processes and enhance patient care by unearthing insights from diverse sources of medical literature and patient data. This not only revolutionizes how care is provided but also redefines patient engagement and information accessibility.

Let's not overlook the realm of **financial services**, where NLP applications parse vast datasets to identify trends, predict market movements, and detect fraudulent activity with uncanny accuracy. Analysts who once relied on intuition and experience now augment decisions with insights derived from NLP-driven analytics, mitigating risks and optimizing decision-making. By automating these analyses, financial institutions can enhance their agility and responsiveness to market dynamics.

In academia and scientific research, NLP tools facilitate the **analysis of scholarly texts**, ensuring researchers stay abreast of the latest developments across a wide swathe of studies. By automating the reading and summarization of journal abstracts or full papers, researchers can devote more time to creative thinking and problem-solving.

Amid these myriad applications, it's important to highlight the array of **development tools and libraries** that have democratized access to NLP technology. Open-source libraries like NLTK, SpaCy, and the Transformers library by Hugging Face offer ready-made structures that developers and researchers can use to build NLP models and applications. These libraries reduce the entry barrier, allowing a wider range of creators to experiment and innovate with language-based data.

These applications and tools are not mere software—they represent a fusion of human linguistic brilliance with artificial acumen, continually learning and adapting as they interweave themselves into our daily lives. Yet, as with any transformative technology, challenges persist. Ethical considerations around privacy, data security, and the potential for bias in NLP decisions underscore the need for responsible development and rigorous oversight.

As NLP applications become more ubiquitous and tools more intricate, they defy the boundaries of pure technology and integrate seamlessly into the cultural fabric of society. They harness language—the very heartbeat of human interaction—and amplify its capacity to connect, persuade, and enlighten, ensuring that machines not only analyze but also complement human intent in increasingly sophisticated ways.

The journey of NLP from theoretical dream to pervasive reality underscores the power of language—and by extension, NLP—to revolutionize industries, transcend limitations, and redefine relationships between technology and humanity. By fostering a deeper understanding of these applications and tools, we are invited to not just observe the digital dance but to choreograph it, steering technology towards more meaningful and inclusive futures.

6.5 Current Challenges in NLP

The landscape of Natural Language Processing (NLP) is a vibrant tapestry woven with unprecedented technological achievements. Yet, as with any burgeoning field, NLP is not without its challenges. Ironically, the very complexities that make human language so enthralling—its nuances, subtleties, and infinite variability—also form the crux of the obstacles facing NLP today. This section delves into these challenges, spotlighting the intricate dance between advancing technology and the limitless depth of linguistic complexity.

At the forefront of these challenges stands **contextual understanding**—the elusive ability to comprehend not just words but the subtleties of situations, tone, and intent that accompany them. Human beings, equipped with an innate sense of context, navigate this effortlessly, understanding sarcasm, irony, or emotion-laden questions without a second thought. However, instruction in such matters doesn't come naturally to machines, whose capabilities hinge on data-driven training rather than lived experience.

A classic example of a contextual challenge involves idiomatic expressions or phrases that derive meaning not from the words themselves but from the cultural or situational subtext they embody. For instance, the English expression "kick the bucket" signifies mortality, a nuance not immediately accessible through a simple word-by-word translation. NLP systems must wrestle with this duality—where words mean more than their constituent letters—a feat requiring vast corpuses of language examples and intricate algorithm design.

Closely related is the hurdle of **ambiguity**. Linguistic ambiguity can occur at various levels: lexical (where words have multiple meanings), syntactic (where sentence structures allow for multiple interpretations), or semantic (where context influences meaning). Consider the sentence, "I saw the man with the telescope." Is it you or the man wielding the telescope? Solving such ambiguities demands a degree of inferential logic and context-awareness that NLP systems continually strive to replicate.

Ambiguity also dovetails with the broader challenge of **polysemy**, where a single word possesses multiple meanings. Just as the word "bank" can represent both a financial institution and a river's edge, NLP models must discern the intended meaning based on context and usage. The task grows daunting as these models confront polysemous vocabularies across languages, necessitating painstaking training or crowdsourced data to inch closer to human-like understanding.

Further complicating matters are the **cultural differences and linguistic diversity** that weave their way through language. Human language is breathtakingly diverse, with over 7,000 languages spoken worldwide, each imbued with its distinct cultural nuances, idioms, and syntactic rules. While advancements have propelled NLP capabilities far beyond simple translation, accurately capturing the cultural essence of speech and text across diverse languages remains a towering challenge.

Consider the delightful complexities inherent in translating humor or poetry, where intent and meaning are tightly interwoven with cultural context. What leaves one audience in stitches might fall flat on another untouched by the original culture's humor paradigm. NLP must navigate these treacherous waters, weaving technology with sensitive cultural awareness to maintain meaning across translations.

The issue of **bias** further complicates the exhilarating march forward in NLP development. Language, a human construct, inherently reflects its creators' biases, conscious or otherwise. As NLP systems learn from vast datasets—collections of existing texts, images, and interactions—they occasionally inherit these biases, spurred by the imperfections of source material. For instance, biased language models may perpetuate stereotypes, misunderstanding groups or subjects based on flawed training material.

Researchers and developers have undertaken the formidable task of not merely recognizing but mitigating these biases. Robust methodologies, from careful dataset selection to evolving oversight mechanisms, are being crafted to confront this challenge. However, the intricacies of bias extension and its nuanced cultural implications remain an ongoing and demanding endeavor.

Adding to the labyrinth of challenges is the **evolution of language itself**. Language is fluid, a living entity forever adapted and shaped by cultural evolution, societal norms, and technological advancements.

Words like "tweet" and "stream" have acquired wholly new meanings within modern digital vernacular. For NLP models, keeping pace with these shifts demands constant updates and educational refinements, akin to teaching an ancient sage the lexicon of each passing generation.

Despite the colossal nature of these challenges, overcoming them hardly represents futility. Instead, they serve as guiding stars, driving relentless innovation and creativity within the NLP spectrum. Each problem domain houses potential solutions—emerging from interdisciplinary research and progressive design principles. More advanced algorithms, increased computational power, and global collaboration converge towards bridging human-machine linguistic gaps effectively.

Moreover, the struggle against these challenges births a stronger foundation for ethical NLP design, as developers actively promote inclusive technology, adaptable to age, culture, and context, respecting and mirroring human linguistic diversity without washing over its vibrant intricacy.

Ultimately, addressing these challenges isn't just about crisp and concise communication between human and machine but about translating the rich vibrancy of human language into a lingua franca understood by technology, enhancing how machines engage with and amplify human potential.

As we face these challenges head-on with curiosity and determination, NLP will continue to evolve into a technological marvel that profoundly enriches how we navigate, understand, and interact with an information-dense universe. In answering these linguistic puzzles, NLP is not merely solving technology's intellectual dilemmas but expanding humanity's horizon, celebrating our shared—and ever-evolving—linguistic tapestry.

Chapter 7

AI in Everyday Life

Artificial Intelligence has seamlessly integrated into everyday life, enhancing convenience and efficiency across various domains. This chapter explores AI's role in personal assistance, smart homes, and transportation, showcasing its impact on daily activities and decision-making processes. It examines how AI-driven devices and applications transform healthcare by improving diagnostics and personalized care. Moreover, the chapter highlights the improvements in consumer services enabled by AI, such as personalized recommendations and automated customer interactions, illustrating the profound influence of AI technologies on the modern lifestyle.

7.1   AI in Personal Assistance

The past few years have witnessed an unprecedented evolution in the way we interact with technology, largely due to the advent of Artificial Intelligence (AI). One of the most significant advancements in this regard is the development of AI-driven personal assistants. Live demonstrations of practical AI applications, they are changing the dynamics of human-computer interaction. Devices such as Siri, Alexa, and Google Assistant have become household staples, evolving from mere novelties to essential facets of our daily lives.

This transformation began with the need to simplify interaction with the increasingly complex digital world. Traditionally, accessing information or executing tasks required clicking through a labyrinthine series of menus or conducting meticulous online searches. AI personal assistants have bridged this gap, performing tasks through voice commands and natural language processing. By examining these technological marvels more deeply, we can gain an appreciation for the sophistication underlying their apparently simple interactions.

To comprehend the current state of AI in personal assistance, it is useful to reflect on their roots. The world caught a glimpse of automated communication with the introduction of simple chatbots decades ago. However, the true leap came with the development of robust natural language processing (NLP) technologies, allowing machines to understand, interpret, and respond to human language as naturally as if speaking to another person. Coupled with advancements in voice recognition software, these tools have set the stage for the emergence of digital assistants.

Siri, Apple's pioneering AI assistant, made its debut in 2011. At the outset, Siri was designed to execute a limited range of tasks: setting alarms, searching the web, or sending messages. Despite its constrained capabilities, Siri became a cultural phenomenon, largely due to its approachable and conversational interface. Siri's playful responses to strange questions only added to its charm, quickly distinguishing it from other forms of technology. It set a precedent, paving the way for more sophisticated AI personal assistants to follow.

Amazon's Alexa pushed this envelope further in 2014. Alexa's innovation lay in its integration with IoT devices, spawning the concept of a smart, interconnected home. By placing Alexa within its Echo devices, Amazon simplified in-home automation, enabling users to control lights, thermostats, and more with mere vocal commands. This integration heralded a new phase of transition, empowering users to operate not just virtual tasks, but physical interfaces within their environments, seamlessly blending AI assistance into the mundane aspects of life.

Google Assistant, launched in 2016, added another dimension by leveraging Google's extensive data and machine learning capabilities. Famed for its analytical prowess, Google Assistant brought context-awareness to the fore, predicting user needs before they were voiced. With its superior web integration, Google Assistant offers insights, reminders, and suggestions that often anticipate user requirements or desires. This predictive approach has marked a qualitative shift in how digital assistants can potentially transcend reactive roles, becoming proactive partners in users' daily routines.

Yet, beyond these technological milestones looms a broader cultural shift. The proliferation of AI personal assistants raises intriguing questions about how we perceive interaction. For many, conversing with a machine that can comprehend and respond to natural language reshapes the notion of dialogue itself. For the first time, technology possesses a semblance of personality, albeit a simulated one. This dynamic often fosters an emotional connection, with users personifying their digital aides as entities with their quirks and traits.

In practical terms, AI personal assistants offer a plethora of benefits. They optimize time management by setting reminders, creating schedules, and notifying users of upcoming commitments. For those who are visually impaired or have mobility challenges, these assistants provide improved access to technology, bridging access gaps and promoting independence. However, the intricacy of these systems lies in their capability to learn and adapt over time, creating personalized experiences based on user habits and preferences. This tailoring process, powered by machine learning algorithms, continually refines interactions and heightens relevance.

One must acknowledge, however, the complexity and privacy implications inherent in the data continuously gathered to fuel these assistants. Every voice command processed by an AI personal assistant is a data point used to enhance its effectiveness but also raises concerns about surveillance and data security. Companies have assured consumers of efforts to anonymize data and strengthen privacy protocols. However, the dialogue surrounding data ethics continues, advocating for transparency and rigorous standards in data handling practices.

The trajectory of AI personal assistants is poised for further transformation. Developments in deep learning and NLP will extend their capabilities, refining understanding, decision-making, and interaction nuances. Future iterations may see these assistants handling more complex tasks, perhaps coordinating aspects of users' professional or personal lives autonomously. The convergence of AI with augmented reality (AR) and virtual reality (VR) could create immersive environments where personal assistants are no longer just voices but visual entities inhabiting digital spaces.

This future opens vistas where digital assistants not only perform tasks but engage in sophisticated dialogues, capturing context not just linguistically but emotionally.

In doing so, they might evolve from functional tools to companions, fostering human connections in an increasingly digital landscape.

AI in personal assistance is thus not merely an exploration of technological capability—it is an examination of possibilities for transforming how we interface with the world around us. As these technologies integrate further into our daily spheres, they stand at the frontier of a new era of interaction, one that enhances human potential while presenting challenges and questions that will shape our technological ethics and culture for years to come.

7.2 Smart Homes and AI

Imagine walking into your home after a long day, and as if by magic, the lights adjust perfectly to your preference, the temperature is set just right, and your favorite music begins to play. This isn't a scene from a science fiction movie; it exemplifies the potential of smart home technology powered by Artificial Intelligence (AI). The emergence of AI in smart homes marks a revolutionary shift in the way we perceive and interact with our living environments, transforming them from static spaces into dynamic hubs of connectivity and automation.

The concept of a smart home is rooted in the idea of interconnected devices working in harmony to simplify and enhance daily living. This isn't entirely new. The seeds were planted in the mid-20th century with the advent of automated systems like thermostats and lawn sprinklers, tailored to improve convenience and efficiency. However, it wasn't until the integration of AI that these systems became truly 'smart,' capable of learning, adapting, and even predicting human behavior.

AI acts as the brain behind the smart home operation. It gathers data from numerous sensors embedded throughout the home and intelligently analyzes this information to recognize patterns and respond to changing environments. This sensory network, often referred to as the Internet of Things (IoT), encompasses everything from refrigerators to security systems, transforming every appliance and device into a node within a broader communicative structure.

A quintessential smart home device is the smart thermostat. Many people have wrestled with the perfect temperature setting, trying to balance comfort and energy efficiency. Enter smart thermostats, equipped with AI algorithms capable of learning household occupancy patterns, personal temperature preferences, and even the most economical energy consumption times. By adapting to these insights, a smart thermostat not only enhances comfort but also cuts energy consumption, benefiting both the user and the environment.

AI's applications within smart homes extend to lighting systems as well. Smart lighting can now adjust based on daylight, room occupancy, and user preferences, creating a balance between energy savings and aesthetic appeal. Imagine entering a room and having the lights adjust to complement natural sunlight or dim to help you unwind in the evening. With AI, lighting systems turn from a mere flick of a switch into an orchestrated ambiance manager.

Home security has also received a substantial upgrade through AI. Smart security systems now boast advanced features such as facial recognition and real-time anomaly detection. Consider the implications: a security system that not only records footage but actively differentiates between family members, guests, and potential intruders. Such technology enhances safety by providing immediate alerts when unexpected incidents occur, allowing for quick responses and peace of mind.

An enticing aspect of AI-driven smart homes lies in their capacity for personal assistance. Beyond routine automation, these systems have the potential to act autonomously, anticipating needs before they are even verbalized. For example, a smart coffee maker might start brewing a cup as it senses you stirring in the morning, or a smart speaker might suggest altering your morning traffic route based on current conditions. These anticipations aren't just convenient; they weave technology into the fabric of daily living in a manner that's seamlessly supportive.

The evolution towards smart homes has not been entirely without challenges. Privacy and data security represent significant concerns, as the same smart devices that make life convenient also gather copious amounts of personal data. Where and how this data is stored and who has access to it are pressing questions. As these systems become more sophisticated, so too must the mechanisms that safeguard the information they collect, emphasizing the ongoing need for robust privacy protections and transparent data policies.

Moreover, the societal impacts of smart homes merit consideration. The technology has the potential to reduce human intervention in many tasks, which could affect employment markets and necessitate new skills training. However, it could also provide tools that promote independence for the elderly or disabled, fostering an improved quality of life.

The future of smart homes is exciting, with AI poised to introduce even more innovative features. Developments in machine learning continue to enhance these systems' predictive capabilities, making them more intuitive and adaptive to human habits and emotions. Picture a home that balances indoor air quality by adjusting ventilation according to pollution levels detected outside, or window blinds that autonomously align with the sun's trajectory to harness optimal natural light. These might sound like dreams today, but they illustrate how AI could transform living spaces into cooperative environments, harmoniously blending nature, technology, and human activity.

Looking further ahead, the role of AI in smart homes may expand to include sustainability initiatives, allowing homes to become actively engaged in resource management and conservation efforts. AI could optimize water usage for irrigation or help manage household waste by suggesting composting or recycling practices. In doing so, these enhancements could contribute to achieving greater ecological consciousness and responsibility.

In bringing homes into the digital age, AI is not just reshaping physical space; it is redefining what it means to make a space a 'home.' It ushers in a future where living environments are adaptive, intelligent, and in tune with their inhabitants, presenting a paradigm where technological advancement is synonymous with a cozy embrace of innovation. As we stand on the brink of this transformation, the potential for AI to redefine domestic life is as limitless as imagination itself, waiting to be realized in the everyday routines of users around the globe.

7.3   AI in Transportation

Transportation, a fundamental element of human civilization, has undergone radical transformations over the centuries—horse-drawn carriages gave way to automobiles, which then evolved into high-speed trains and aircraft. Today, we stand at the brink of yet another revolution, with Artificial Intelligence (AI) playing a pivotal role in reimagining how we move. AI in transportation not only offers enhancements in efficiency and safety, but it also has the potential to redefine the very concept of mobility altogether.

The integration of AI into transportation systems is not an isolated phenomenon; rather, it builds on centuries of innovation aimed at improving how we travel. The early 20th century, for example, saw the introduction of traffic signals—a primitive yet profound precursor to intelligent transport systems. These signals dictated traffic flow long before the idea of smart cities was conceived. Fast forward to the present, the notion of AI-assisted transportation embodies this same ethos—elevating coordination and efficiency to previously unimaginable standards.

A critical component of AI in transportation is machine learning, particularly its subset, deep learning. These technologies allow systems to analyze massive datasets, recognize patterns, and make decisions faster and more accurately than a human ever could. Take GPS navigation, an AI application many of us use almost daily. It has evolved from basic route plotting to real-time updates on traffic congestion, accident warnings, and even suggestions for optimal traveling times. These insights are possible through AI's ability to process information from countless sources, including satellite data, traffic cameras, and historical travel patterns.

However, the most transformative aspect of AI in transportation is undoubtedly autonomous vehicles. Whether it be cars, trucks, or drones, the idea of machines navigating complex environments is almost magical, promising to change our roads and skies forever. Companies like Tesla, Waymo, and Uber are at the forefront of this innovation, with self-driving cars that blend a vast array of AI technologies, such as computer vision, radar, lidar, and GPS, into a cohesive system capable of executing flawless driving tasks.

The potential benefits of autonomous vehicles are enormous. They could profoundly reduce traffic accidents—human error is responsible for the majority of crashes—and thus save countless lives. Additionally, these vehicles present solutions to inefficiencies such as traffic congestion and unnecessary emissions. Imagine a fleet of AI-driven taxis that coordinate with one another to maximize ride-sharing, reduce road usage, and lower pollution levels simultaneously.

Yet, as groundbreaking as autonomous vehicles promise to be, they are not without challenges. These involve not only technical hurdles in ensuring foolproof safety but also ethical dilemmas. For instance, how should a car programmed to minimize harm act when faced with an unavoidable accident? These moral quandaries invite philosophical debates that blend technology and ethics in unprecedented ways.

Beyond private transport, AI's footprint in public transportation systems is gaining ground. Cities are investing in AI-driven buses and trains that adjust their schedules and routes based on real-time demands, alleviating peak-time bottlenecks. London's public transport system, for example, uses AI to predict passenger flows, optimizing service delivery and reducing waiting times. Ultimately, AI transforms public transportation systems into adaptive networks capable of responding dynamically to the demands of urban life.

Furthermore, AI's influence extends to freight and logistics. AI-driven algorithms optimize delivery routes, balance loads, and even gauge the health of logistics fleets. This optimization streamlines operations, reduces costs, and minimizes the industry's carbon footprint, a prime concern in our climate-aware society. Companies like Amazon and DHL tirelessly leverage AI to increase operational efficiency, enabling faster delivery times and enhancing customer satisfaction.

In air travel, AI is ushering innovations ranging from flight scheduling and maintenance prediction to the efficient management of air traffic control. Predictive analytics—one of AI's standout features—enables airlines to not only predict mechanical failures before they happen but also to fine-tune fuel usage during flights, saving money and reducing emissions. Further, AI's sophisticated data analytics provide insights into passenger preferences, enabling personalized travel experiences.

AI's implementation in transport is not restricted to vehicles and logistics alone. It also manifests through the development of smart infrastructure. Roads with embedded sensors communicate with vehicles to provide updates about traffic conditions, enhance navigation systems, and even assist in instantaneous accident detection and emergency response. Urban centers that invest in such intelligent infrastructure promise to reduce friction between various transportation modes, leading to smoother transit experiences.

While the technological frontier of AI in transportation is breathtaking, we must remain vigilant about its consequences. Privacy is a significant concern as data collection is central to AI's efficacy. Balancing convenience and security requires stringent regulations and policies to protect user data from misuse.

Furthermore, the social implications of AI-driven transport systems demand careful scrutiny. As traditional roles within the transport sector evolve—be it truck drivers, taxi operators, or road maintenance crews—there's a genuine risk of workforce displacement. Preparing for such shifts will entail investment in retraining programs and educational modules that equip individuals for new roles within an AI-enhanced transport ecosystem.

As we steer towards an AI-driven future, the horizon of possibilities in transportation promises a realm where mobility is efficient, safe, and aligned with the broader goals of sustainability and urban development. Autonomous vehicles, smart infrastructure, and predictive logistics systems are just the beginning of a profound evolution shaped by AI's relentless drive towards innovation.

Thus, AI in transportation encapsulates much more than technological advancement—it symbolizes humanity's enduring quest to refine and perfect the art of movement itself. In doing so, it not only reshapes how we traverse the earth but also challenges us to reconsider what it means to journey, be it across town or around the globe.

7.4   AI in Healthcare

Artificial intelligence (AI) is rapidly emerging as a transformative force within the healthcare industry, a sector where precision and timely intervention can drastically alter outcomes. The application of AI in healthcare distills the art of diagnostics, treatment, and patient care, marrying cutting-edge technology with the nuanced complexities of human health. While the notion of machines assisting in medical procedures might evoke images of sci-fi futures, the reality presents a nuanced collaboration where technology acts as an ally in the quest for wellbeing.

The historical journey leading to AI's integration in healthcare is one traceable through the gradual convergence of data and technology. The late 20th century saw the proliferation of electronic health records—an innovation that transformed patient data into a digital goldmine. By compiling extensive collections of medical histories, treatment outcomes, and genetic information, healthcare systems unknowingly laid the foundations for today's AI applications. This accumulation of data now fuels AI's analytical potential, unlocking insights previously obscured in layers of analog records.

One of the most groundbreaking applications of AI in healthcare is diagnostic aid. Traditional medical diagnostics often relied heavily on the experience and intuition of healthcare professionals—a process inherently prone to human error. AI steps in to refine this process through image recognition and pattern analysis. For instance, AI algorithms in radiology can sift through vast volumes of imaging data—X-rays, MRIs, CT scans—and accurately identify anomalies such as tumors, often with greater precision than a human eye. This assistance not only accelerates diagnostic processes but often catches inconsistencies that might elude even seasoned practitioners.

Take, for example, DeepMind's AI, which has demonstrated remarkable success in diagnosing eye diseases by interpreting retinal scans. Such capabilities are poised to revolutionize ophthalmology, not only by speeding up diagnostics but also by increasing accessibility to care, especially in regions where specialists are scarce.

159

However, diagnostics is just one area in which AI promises significant innovations. Personalized medicine, which tailors treatment to the individual characteristics of each patient, has gained substantial momentum due to AI. By analyzing genetic information, lifestyle factors, and ongoing health data, AI systems can predict how patients might react to different therapies, allowing doctors to devise the most effective treatment plans. The potential to anticipate drug interactions, mitigate side effects, and customize pharmaceuticals could usher in a new era of precision healthcare, transforming how individuals receive medical care.

AI's prowess for pattern recognition also extends into another crucial facet of healthcare—predictive analytics. By leveraging big data, AI models can foresee potential health trends by identifying patterns within populations. Such predictive capabilities are invaluable for public health planning, enabling authorities to brace for outbreaks, allocate resources optimally, or preemptively address looming health crises.

Additionally, AI is reshaping the surgical landscape through robotics. Surgical robots equipped with AI algorithms can perform intricate procedures with a level of precision and steadiness that far surpasses human capabilities. These robots act not as substitutes but as extended arms of the surgeons, enhancing their dexterity and allowing for minimally invasive procedures. The outcomes are shorter recovery times, reduced trauma for patients, and higher surgical success rates. Robotic surgery systems such as the da Vinci Surgical System are already a staple in many operating rooms worldwide, conducting procedures ranging from cardiac surgery to urology.

Moreover, AI's impact is palpable in streamlining administrative tasks, a perennial pain point in healthcare systems. Natural language processing algorithms can transcribe patient visits, update electronic health records, and manage billing systems—all tasks traditionally consuming significant time. By harnessing AI for these menial but necessary operations, healthcare providers can refocus efforts on patient care, reducing burnout and improving practitioner satisfaction.

Mingling AI with healthcare, however, is not merely a tale of triumphs; it poses challenges that warrant meticulous examination. Ethical questions, for instance, loom large. The idea of machines assuming roles traditionally reserved for human caregivers raises concerns about machine reliance and the potential for depersonalized care. Furthermore, errors in AI systems—though infrequent—can have profound ramifications, necessitating strict validation and monitoring protocols.

Privacy is another cornerstone issue as AI applications rely heavily on personal data. Amidst growing concerns about data security, achieving patient trust hinges on transparent data practices and robust security measures. Ensuring that sensitive health data remains confidential demands collaborations between technologists, policymakers, and healthcare professionals to establish stringent safeguards.

Yet, these challenges do not eclipse the vast potential AI holds in democratizing healthcare. Its deployment can transcend urban-rural divides, delivering quality healthcare to under-resourced areas. Telemedicine platforms, enhanced with AI diagnostics, could redefine care delivery across continents, providing expert-level consultations remotely and reducing the need for costly travel.

AI is also fostering interdisciplinary collaborations, spurring innovations that blur the lines separating medicine, engineering, and computer science. These

161

synergies illuminate new paths for exploration—whether in developing wearable devices that monitor health indicators or creating AI systems capable of understanding complex disease mechanisms at a molecular level.

In reflecting on AI's role in healthcare, one is reminded of the underlying mission of medicine—to enhance human life. AI amplifies this mission, offering tools that can enhance diagnostic accuracy, optimize treatment, and streamline processes. It is an enabler, not a replacement, of human ingenuity and compassion. Bridging technology and medicine presents unique challenges and unparalleled opportunities, mirroring the fast-evolving landscape of healthcare itself.

As AI continues to integrate into healthcare, its potential applications are as boundless as the imagination of those who dare to innovate and explore. In the narrative of human health and wellbeing, the AI chapter has only just begun, shading the promise of a future where healthcare not only becomes more efficient and accessible but also fundamentally more human through the enhancement of compassion and care.

7.5 Consumer Services Enhanced by AI

Imagine entering a café, and before you reach the counter, your smartphone quietly vibrates, presenting a notification: your favorite drink is being prepared just the way you like it, identified through your previous orders and mood from calendar events. Welcome to the world where AI, or Artificial Intelligence, enriches consumer services in ways that blur the lines between personalization and prescience. Across industries, AI is crafting new paradigms in consumer interaction, enhancing convenience, personal connection, and satisfaction on an unprecedented scale.

The use of AI in consumer services stems from the quest to understand customer preferences and behavior more deeply, drawing a line back to the dawn of commerce, where traders thrived by discerning their customers' desires and tailoring their offerings accordingly. The more things change, the more they stay the same: today's AI technologies carry this tradition forward at a speed and scale that were previously unimaginable.

The e-commerce industry has been particularly fertile ground for AI innovations. Retail giants like Amazon use AI algorithms to analyze purchase habits and browsing histories, creating personalized shopping experiences that are both intuitive and anticipatory. You might conclude a browsing session for hiking gear only to discover tailored recommendations in your inbox that align perfectly with your interests, a functionality powered by AI's ability to process vast datasets and discern patterns of routine and anomaly.

AI's capabilities extend well beyond recommendation engines. Chatbots, powered by natural language processing, have transformed customer service, offering round-the-clock assistance without the wait times traditionally associated with human operators. These digital assistants can manage a spectrum of enquiries— from providing product information to resolving complaints—while continuously learning from previous interactions to improve response accuracy and relevance. The efficiency of chatbots stems not just from their tireless ability to field questions, but from their potential to develop deep learning models that help anticipate customer intent.

Streaming services like Netflix and Spotify also capitalize on AI to refine user experiences. By leveraging sophisticated recommendation algorithms, these platforms don't merely suggest content—they create pathways through a vast thicket of media, acting as curators for particular tastes and even nudging viewers or listeners toward new interests. This capability stems from AI's knack for clustering user behavior data and applying it to predict what audiences might want next, ensuring platforms remain ever engaging.

Retail and streaming experiences are not where AI's consumer service enhancement story ends. The travel and hospitality industry is also undergoing a tech-inspired metamorphosis. AI-enhanced platforms equip travelers with itineraries adjusted in real-time based on variables such as weather changes, local events, or flight disruptions. Virtual assistants can book travel accommodations tailored to personal preferences and budget considerations, often communicating seamlessly across languages and currencies—thus taking the hassle out of planning and enabling travelers to focus on the journey.

The hospitality sector has introduced AI-driven concierge services in hotels, offering personalized experiences that cater to the specific needs and desires of guests. From room settings pre-configured to your liking before you even check in, to automated checkouts, AI optimally translates data into service that adds comfort and convenience without compromising on warmth and hospitality.

Beyond these conveniences, AI is making headway in more niche areas like fashion through virtual try-ons, where consumers can visualize clothing fit and style from the comfort of their home. AI algorithms analyze body measurements and personal style cues to suggest clothing that complements a shopper's physique and preferences. These systems save time and enhance shopping confidence, bridging the gap between online and physical retail experiences.

The potential of AI in consumer services often invites us to dream about the fine line between eerily predictive technology and helpful suggestion. But as with all revolutions, this remarkable capacity for personalization comes with significant questions and challenges. Privacy concerns loom large, as personalized experiences rely heavily on accumulating and analyzing personal data. The boundaries of acceptable data usage and the ethics around AI decision-making remain central debates within this landscape. Transparency—in how data is collected, analyzed, and utilized—becomes pivotal in maintaining consumer trust and fostering responsible AI deployment.

Moreover, there is an underlying societal ramification regarding AI's role in consumer services: the potential displacement of human jobs. Just as chatbots now handle queries once fielded by customer service representatives, the continued evolution of AI might risk underemployment in sectors that involve routine tasks. Addressing these challenges will require a multidimensional response—balancing technological advancement with human focused policies, fostering skills development, and envisioning new roles AI itself might create.

AI's potential to streamline consumer services is nothing short of transformative. It brings a confluence where intuition meets intelligence, reducing friction in consumer journeys, and enhancing the quality of everyday experiences. Businesses that skillfully leverage AI stand to strengthen their competitive edge, offering products and services that do not simply meet needs but anticipate them with exceptional precision.

As AI continues to refine consumer services, it is responsible for creating ecosystems of efficiency where human involvement and algorithmic decision-making blur seamlessly, working together as two halves of a coherent whole. The future promises more adaptive, intuitive consumer interactions—groundbreaking developments that lie just over the digital horizon. In this landscape, technology does not replace the human touch; rather, it refines and amplifies it, offering consumers a world where engagement is not just transactional, but relational and vibrant.

The journey of AI in enhancing consumer services thus mirrors an ongoing saga of evolution, anchored in the eternal pursuit of understanding the human experience and enriching it with technological advances. As we stand at the crossroads of AI's possibilities and its ethical intricacies, embracing this duality becomes vital—a challenge and an opportunity to craft future consumer experiences that are as thoughtful as they are innovative. In this delicate balance lies the masterful potential to create a world where the conveniences of tomorrow are shaped by both savvy algorithms and sagacious humanity.

Chapter 8

Ethics and AI: Navigating Challenges

The ethical implications of Artificial Intelligence are critical considerations as technology advances and permeates more aspects of life. This chapter examines key ethical issues, including privacy concerns and data security, emphasizing the need for responsible AI use and development. It explores the challenges of addressing biases and ensuring fairness within AI systems, highlighting the importance of transparency and accountability in automated decision-making. The chapter also discusses regulatory efforts and ethical guidelines that aim to safeguard the integrity of AI technologies, ensuring they are developed and deployed in a manner that aligns with societal values and norms.

8.1   Understanding AI Ethics

Artificial Intelligence (AI) has been described as the driving force of the new industrial revolution, a phenomenon seemingly capable of transforming every facet of our daily existence.   While the excitement surrounding AI is palpable, it comes with a Pandora's box of ethical concerns. These concerns stem from the way AI is developed and utilized, impacting facets of fairness, transparency, accountability, and our very understanding of autonomy and privacy.

At a fundamental level, AI ethics revolves around evaluating the moral implications of AI systems in real-world applications. It invites us to consider: How do we ensure that AI technologies are not only effective but also equitable and respectful of human values? Let us embark on a journey through the ethical labyrinth that surrounds AI, an exploration that will draw from historical philosophical quandaries and contemporary technological dilemmas alike.

AI and Moral Philosophy

To unpack AI ethics, we must momentarily step into the realm of moral philosophy. Traditionally, ethics has been concerned with the principles of right and wrong behavior. In AI, we encounter ethical questions that are reminiscent of age-old debates, now infused with the complexity of machine decision-making.

Consider the ethical framework of utilitarianism, which advocates for actions that maximize happiness or well-being. One might argue that an AI system designed to optimize healthcare outcomes based on utilitarian principles is inherently ethical. Yet, this approach might inadvertently neglect minority groups whose needs do not align with the majority. Here, AI ethics challenges us to navigate the dichotomy between collective benefits and individual rights, a reminder of the tension found in Bentham's greatest happiness principle.

Deontological ethics, championed by Immanuel Kant, offers another lens. It emphasizes duties and rules, suggesting that actions are ethical if they align with

168

a predefined set of ethical duties, regardless of the consequences. AI systems programmed to comply with strict legalities might appear ethical deontologically but may still fall short in moral nuance, failing to capture the richness and flexibility of human ethical decision-making.

The Fairness Conundrum

Fairness, a cornerstone of ethical AI, invites heated debate. An AI system is considered fair if it does not favor one individual or group over another. However, achieving fairness is easier said than done. Algorithms trained on biased data can, unintentionally, perpetuate or amplify societal biases. A facial recognition system with accuracy disparities across different racial groups showcases this pitfall. As a result, AI ethics calls for vigilance to ensure that these systems are designed and monitored to mitigate bias.

The emerging field of Fairness, Accountability, and Transparency (FAccT) promotes methods for assessing and correcting biases in AI. These range from process oversight in algorithm design to auditing outputs and ensuring diverse representation in training data sets. Nevertheless, the complexities of human fairness and justice continue to challenge even the best algorithms.

Transparency: The Crystal Ball of AI

Transparency in AI is akin to the clarity one seeks when peering into a crystal ball. Users and stakeholders must understand how AI systems reach decisions to trust them meaningfully. Yet, many AI models, especially those categorized as "black boxes," operate with opaqueness, making interpretability difficult.

Consider the example of a machine learning model used for credit scoring. Consumers denied credit may not be privy to the reasoning, remaining in the dark about how factors were weighted. Transparency initiatives, such as providing explanation interfaces or implementing simpler, interpretable models, aim to demystify these processes.

However, transparency also exposes underlying intricacies—detailing models to the uninitiated might not lead to understanding but rather confusion or misinformation. Thus, AI ethics emphasizes balancing openness with intelligibility, avoiding the trap of overloading users with technically dense descriptions.

Accountability: Who Holds the Reins?

Accountability in AI is about determining who is responsible when things go awry. As AI systems become complex and autonomous, attributing accountability can feel like a game of musical chairs where the music never stops.

For instance, self-driving cars challenge traditional notions of driver accountability. Should responsibility lie with the manufacturer, the software developer, or some other party? AI ethics pushes for a more nuanced examination of liability chains, advocating for clear policies and robust governance structures to determine who should answer for AI actions.

The concept of "human-in-the-loop" is a proposed safeguard mechanism, ensuring that critical or contentious decisions are overseen by human judgment. Yet, given the growing sophistication of AI, the balance between machine autonomy and human oversight requires continuous re-evaluation.

Autonomy and Consent in the Age of AI

AI systems have the potential to influence personal choices, raising questions about autonomy and informed consent. Consider personalized recommendation systems on streaming platforms: they shape viewing habits, subtly nudging choices in particular directions. While seemingly benign, they raise ethical questions about the erosion of autonomous decision-making.

Moreover, AI's ability to predict behavior poses privacy concerns. Deep learning models can infer sensitive information from seemingly innocuous data—reflecting on how our data should be collected, stored, and used, the ethical debate centers on individual consent and data ownership.

In numerous jurisdictions, regulations such as the General Data Protection Regulation (GDPR) enforce stricter controls over data use, embedding ethical considerations into legal frameworks. However, as AI evolves, so too must our interpretations of autonomy and consent, challenging both policymakers and ethicists to keep pace with technological advancements.

The Road Ahead: Ethics By Design

Embedding ethics within AI technologies from inception is imperative. This "ethics by design" approach necessitates interdisciplinary collaboration inclusive of technologists, ethicists, sociologists, and the public. It urges continuous dialogue rather than seeing ethics as a checklist to comply with.

The development of AI Ethics Boards in organizations, transparent public consultations, and the integration of ethical foresight in AI curricula are steps forward. Yet, the fluid nature of technology requires adaptable frameworks, ready to address emerging ethical considerations that continue to surface.

Understanding AI ethics is akin to navigating a terrain marked by both exciting prospects and formidable challenges. It is a realm where historical ethical theories intersect dynamically with modern technological realities, urging us to uphold human values as steadfast beacons. As we press onward into the era of AI, embracing a conscientious, committed, and comprehensive approach to ethics matters not just for the technology we create but, fundamentally, for the society we wish to flourish.

8.2 Privacy and Data Security

Picture a world where every click, tap, or swipe leaves a digital breadcrumb, a trail of your existence weaving through the vast expanse of cyberspace. This might sound like the plot of a futuristic thriller, yet it is hardly an exaggeration of our current reality. Artificial Intelligence (AI), while enabling unprecedented possibilities, intensifies the pressing discourse on privacy and data security. The intertwining of these elements with AI demands our scrutiny, evoking questions about how we protect our information and preserve privacy in a data-driven age.

At its core, privacy refers to the right of individuals to control their personal information and safeguard it from unwarranted intrusion. Data security, on the other hand, involves the technical measures and ethical practices employed to protect data from breaches and misuse. As AI systems consume copious amounts of data to deliver tailored experiences and drive innovation, the conversation around privacy and data security becomes ever more critical.

The roots of today's privacy concerns trace back to an era predating the digital revolution. Take the census, for instance, an ancient exercise dating back to Babylonia over 3800 years ago, conceived to count populations for taxation and governance. Privacy, as we understand it, was scarcely a consideration. Fast forward to the Information Age, and the scales have tipped dramatically. The exponential growth in data, tirelessly harvested by AI and algorithms, has amplified the conversation around privacy.

In today's AI-driven landscape, data collection is omnipresent. Every digital interaction generates data, which AI solutions leverage to enhance user experiences—be it personalizing advertisements, customizing news feeds, or recommending products. However, the same data that enhances our digital encounters can become a double-edged sword when it falls into the wrong hands.

Consider, for example, smart home devices like voice-activated assistants. These technological marvels offer convenience but at a cost: constant data streaming and storage. Where do we draw the line between convenience and intrusion? This question echoes in the digital corridors as we navigate a world where privacy risks encroach upon our autonomy.

One notable consequence of rampant data collection is the potential for surveillance. Our digital behavior, meticulously catalogued by AI, provides insights into habits, preferences, and vulnerabilities. While these insights are invaluable for businesses seeking to understand consumer behavior, they also pose significant privacy threats. Instances of unauthorized surveillance by both corporations and governments stoke fears of an Orwellian dystopia—a slippery slope AI enthusiasts and ethicists are keenly aware of.

Moreover, data privacy breaches can be catastrophic, affecting millions. Akin to pirates boarding a ship and plundering its cargo, malicious actors exploit vulnerabilities to access sensitive data. This data, ranging from credit card information to medical records, can lead to identity theft, financial losses, and reputational damage.

While breaches and surveillance are overt threats, more insidious is the illusion of consent that pervades digital services. When was the last time you diligently read through a service agreement before hastily clicking "I Agree"? This routine act implicating consent is often a façade, eroding genuine autonomy.

In AI, consent becomes particularly convoluted. Machine learning models rely on vast datasets, prompting questions about how this data is acquired and whether users are adequately informed. This is where ethical AI practices and regulations come into play, ensuring that consent is informed, explicit, and regularly updated.

Regulations like the General Data Protection Regulation (GDPR) in the European Union signify strides in fortifying data privacy. Built on principles of transparency, accountability, and user rights, GDPR mandates organizations to maintain robust data protection protocols. However, these regulations are not without their challenges, as rapidly evolving AI technologies continue to test their boundaries.

Data security, the fortification that protects our digital treasures, hinges on the practice of encrypting information, rendering it unintelligible to unauthorized users. Encryption, a process as old as Julius Caesar's substitution cipher, is crucial in our digital age. It ensures that even if data is intercepted, it remains inaccessible without the proper decryption keys.

In the AI ecosystem, encryption fulfills a dual purpose: safeguarding data during transmission and storing the results of AI analyses securely. Modern encryption algorithms like AES (Advanced Encryption Standard) provide robust defense mechanisms, integrating seamlessly into AI workflows to ensure data integrity.

However, encryption alone is not a panacea. Effective data security requires a holistic approach that encompasses various measures including multi-factor authentication, regular security audits, and rapid response strategies to mitigate potential threats.

Balancing AI innovation with privacy and data security is akin to walking a tightrope. AI's potential thrives upon data—without it, machine learning models would lack the lifeblood to learn and improve. Nonetheless, this ceaseless pursuit of information must not overshadow the fundamental right to privacy.

Innovative solutions like differential privacy have emerged, allowing AI systems to glean insights from datasets without compromising individual privacy. By injecting statistical "noise" into data, differential privacy masks individual identities while enabling robust data analysis. Similarly, federated learning presents a promising paradigm, wherein AI models are trained locally on devices rather than centralized data repositories, reducing risks associated with data transfer and storage.

These approaches underscore the possibility of smart, privacy-preserving AI—a testament to the brilliance of innovation that addresses ethical quandaries. Yet, implementing such solutions requires rigorous scientific effort and often confronts resistance from entities accustomed to unfettered data access.

The pathway to reconciling privacy with AI advancement lies in establishing ethical AI governance. This involves drafting comprehensive data policies, promoting transparency in AI operations, and fostering a culture of accountability. Institutions and organizations must be proactive, adopting best practices for data management and security to anticipate challenges rather than react to crises.

Ethical AI governance is inherently collaborative, involving policymakers, technologists, ethicists, and consumers in continual dialogue. Such partnerships are crucial to developing adaptive regulations that remain relevant amidst technological progress.

Furthermore, public awareness and education initiatives play a pivotal role, empowering individuals to make informed decisions about their digital footprints. Privacy literacy enables consumers to advocate for their rights, fostering a climate where respect for privacy is integral to technological ecosystems.

The intersection of privacy, data security, and AI is a dynamic and intricate arena. It demands a delicate balance between reaping the benefits of data-driven AI and preserving the sanctity of privacy. Our journey through this landscape is ongoing, guided by the principles of ethical consideration and conscientious innovation. As we navigate this path, let us remain vigilant custodians of our digital domain, ensuring that privacy and security are not casualties in the march toward technological progress.

8.3   Bias and Fairness in AI

Could an algorithm be prejudiced? At first glance, this might sound paradoxical. Machines, after all, lack consciousness—they don't harbor opinions, beliefs, or biases, right? Yet, as artificial intelligence (AI) increasingly shapes critical aspects of our lives, from job recruitment to law enforcement, questions of bias and fairness in AI systems come to the forefront. Understanding and addressing these concerns is crucial to ensuring that AI technologies serve all members of society equitably.

AI's capacity for bias does not stem from any innate qualities of the technology itself but rather from the data it processes and the humans who design and train these systems. Embedded within mountains of data are societal inequities and historical prejudices, which, when left unchecked, can translate into skewed AI decisions. Delve with us into the complexities of bias in AI, its historical background, examples of its impact, and strategies to promote fairness.

A Glimpse into History: Bias Beyond Machines

While AI is a modern marvel, bias is an age-old human flaw. Historical biases—rooted in culture, traditions, or prejudices—have influenced societal structures and individual interactions for millennia. Think of how biases informed policies like segregation or redlining, creating systemic inequalities that have lingered across generations.

As AI learns from human-generated data, it inherits these past injustices, perpetuating them if left unchecked. Consider the 19th-century phrenology practices, where pseudoscientific methods concluded intelligence based on skull shape—a bias that unfoundedly influenced societal perceptions and decisions. Fast forward to today, AI's reliance on historical data can mean these outdated biases resurface in automated forms, sometimes unbeknownst to users or developers.

When Algorithms Show Favoritism

Artificial intelligence, for all its promises of objectivity and precision, is like a mirror reflecting the data from which it learns. If that data is biased, the resultant AI decisions will likely be biased, too. Here are a few infamous instances of algorithmic bias that prompt a closer examination.

One often-cited case involved facial recognition technology, which was found to have significantly lower accuracy in identifying individuals with darker skin tones compared to lighter-skinned individuals. This disparity arose because the datasets primarily contained light-skinned faces, highlighting a lack of diversity that skewed algorithmic performance.

Another striking example involves AI used in judicial settings. In some systems designed to predict criminal recidivism, studies found that black defendants were more likely to receive higher risk scores than their white counterparts with similar profiles. Such biases arise not just from the datasets but also from subjective human decisions baked into algorithmic models.

These examples underscore an uncomfortable truth: when AI systems exhibit bias, they can reinforce or even exacerbate existing inequalities, leading to real-world consequences that demand urgent attention and action.

Decoding Bias: Understanding Its Origins

Algorithmic bias can manifest through several pathways, often subtly woven into AI systems during the data curation and algorithm design processes. Here are a few key origins of bias in AI:

- **Data Bias**: AI systems rely on massive datasets to learn patterns and make predictions. If these datasets are not representative of the population or context they intend to serve, the models may skew toward the prevailing majority, marginalizing underrepresented groups.

- **Pre-existing Bias**: Historical prejudices embedded within data can resurface in AI models. When trained on such data, AI systems may inadvertently perpetuate societal stereotypes and biases.

- **Algorithmic Bias**: Beyond data, the algorithms and model designs themselves can introduce bias. If a model prioritizes certain objectives over fairness, or if biased assumptions guide its construction, bias can ensue.

- **Interaction Bias**: The way users interact with AI systems can also introduce bias. For example, if a particular algorithm is more favorable to one demographic, users may unknowingly reinforce and exacerbate that bias through repeated interactions.

Ensuring Fairness: Strategies for Equitable AI

To mitigate bias and champion fairness, we must adopt a multifaceted approach that combines technical solutions with ethical considerations and regulatory oversight. Here are some strategies that can help navigate the bias-fairness conundrum:

- **Diversifying Datasets**: Ensuring that training data is representative and inclusive of diverse groups is vital. Efforts should be made to source data from various demographics and cultural contexts, reducing skew and enhancing fairness.

- **Bias Audits and Impact Assessments**: Regularly auditing AI systems for bias is crucial to identify and address disparities. These audits can help developers understand where and how bias enters, enabling them to create more equitable solutions.

179

- **Fairness-Aware Algorithms**: Implementing fairness constraints within algorithmic models can help achieve balanced outcomes. Techniques such as adversarial debiasing and fairness constraints can assist in counteracting biased tendencies.

- **Human Oversight and Transparency**: Establishing frameworks for human oversight ensures that AI systems do not function unchecked. Transparency mandates, such as explicability and open access to decision-making processes, can foster trust and accountability.

- **Regulatory Frameworks and Guidelines**: Governments and international bodies play a significant role by establishing standards and regulations to enforce fairness in AI. Policies addressing ethical AI practices set the stage for systematic, industry-wide improvements.

- **Interdisciplinary Collaboration**: Bridging the gap between technologists, ethicists, sociologists, and users ensures a holistic approach to AI development. Collaborative efforts allow diverse perspectives to identify ethical blind spots and foster innovation.

A Glimpse Into the Future: Building Ethical AI

As we look toward the future, the challenge lies not only in recognizing bias in AI systems but in systematically dismantling it. The quest for fair AI is ongoing, integrating ethical foresight into development protocols and fostering inclusive innovation. It demands that we remain vigilant, anticipating new biases that arise as technology and society evolve.

AI holds the potential to transcend human limitations,

opening new realms of possibility. To harness this potential responsibly, we must commit to principles of fairness, prioritizing approaches that are just and equitable. In doing so, we ensure that AI systems amplify human capabilities, serving all individuals with dignity and respect.

Bias and fairness in AI represent a complex yet vital conversation—a narrative that interlaces ethics with technological progress. By creating systems attuned to fairness, we take significant steps towards a future where AI reflects the brilliance of human aspirations, unfettered by the shadows of our historical prejudices. Let this be our collective call to action: to champion AI that uplifts, empowers, and reflects the diversity and equality of the world it seeks to enhance.

8.4 Accountability and Transparency

In the journey through the dazzling realm of artificial intelligence (AI), two critical signposts guide the ethical development and deployment of these technologies: accountability and transparency. Much like the person holding the map in a great expedition, without accountability, we may find ourselves in a quagmire where mistakes are frequent, and lessons are scarce. Transparency, on the other hand, acts as our beacon, shedding light on the murky processes within the complex algorithms that govern AI systems.

Together, accountability and transparency ensure that AI operates within the confines of ethical standards and societal norms. They enable us to build trust, foster trustworthiness, and illuminate the often-invisible mechanisms that drive AI decisions. Let us explore how history, practical examples, and current strategies intertwine to create a robust framework designed to uphold these principles in AI.

Historical Context: The Roots of Transparency and Accountability

Long before our fascination with silicon processors and neural networks, accountability and transparency were essential components of societal structures. History illustrates how these values have been pivotal in governance, commerce, and communal interactions. From the time of the Magna Carta in 1215, which set longstanding precedents for transparency through documented agreements, to the expectation of financial accountability in the Wall Street of the 20th century, these principles have served as cornerstones of organized, ethical operations.

In the context of AI, accountability involves determining who is responsible for AI-driven actions. Transparency ensures stakeholders understand and are informed about how AI systems function—akin to demanding the board game instructions before embarking on a highly strategic match. As AI systems are often designed to perform deep, complex analyses that may seem opaque to outsiders, advocating clarity is not just beneficial but necessary.

The Crucial Need for Accountability in AI

Imagine an autonomous vehicle navigating city streets. Its AI-driven system analyzes real-time data inputs, making split-second decisions that could mean the difference between a smooth drive and a fender bender. In the event of a malfunction or accident, who bears the responsibility? This scenario illustrates the pressing need for accountability in AI-driven decisions.

Accountability ensures that entities deploying AI systems are answerable for their outcomes. It challenges us to delineate clear lines of responsibility among developers, manufacturers, and users. This is particularly complex in AI, where decision-making is often distributed across algorithms supported by vast, interwoven datasets. The liability chains become intricate, sometimes indecipherable.

Accountability in AI demands an understanding of how decisions are made and a commitment to uphold ethical standards. Failure to ensure accountability risks causing harm, eroding public trust, and preventing the adoption of innovative technologies. Legal accountability frameworks need to adapt rapidly, keeping pace with the blazing speed of AI advancement and safeguarding individuals from potential harm.

Proposals like implementing AI "kill switches" for emergency halting of operations illustrate accountability strategies, as do rigorous validation and verification processes that ensure AI systems adhere to ethical standards before deployment.

Shedding Light: Transparency as an Essential AI Ingredient

Transparency in AI is akin to lifting the curtain, revealing the wizard conjuring magic. It involves elucidating the decision-making processes and providing insights into how AI systems operate. This illumination of the inner workings aids developers, regulators, and users in understanding, trusting, and evaluating AI outputs.

Consider the medical industry, where AI systems offer diagnostic assistance. For healthcare professionals to effectively utilize AI recommendations, transparency is vital. Understanding how an AI reaches a diagnosis allows practitioners to evaluate its validity, ensuring patient safety and care quality. The clarity that transparency offers not only builds trust but also

183

facilitates systemic improvement, as insights into AI decision-making may reveal areas where the model could be fine-tuned or redesigned.

A crucial element of transparency is explainability or interpretability. An AI system is transparent if it can provide human-understandable insights into the rationale behind its decisions. Think of explainability as akin to a chef disclosing the recipe for a signature dish—revealing key ingredients, steps, and nuances that can be evaluated, critiqued, or replicated.

Balancing the Scales: Challenges Ahead

However, achieving accountability and transparency in AI is no mere feat. The path is strewn with challenges that must be met with nuanced approaches.

- **Complexity of AI Systems**: AI algorithms, especially deep learning models, often operate as intricate "black boxes." Extracting insights from these systems can be laborious, with their sophisticated architecture posing interpretability challenges.

- **Proprietary Interests**:   Companies developing AI technologies might be reluctant to disclose details about their algorithms, fearing intellectual property theft or competitive disadvantage. This hinders efforts to promote transparency.

- **Legal and Ethical Ambiguities**:   Navigating accountability in AI involves confronting legal and ethical uncertainties.   Traditional legal frameworks might not neatly apply to AI contexts, necessitating avant-garde regulatory approaches.

- **User Understanding**: Ensuring that transparency efforts are successful requires that they are accessible and comprehensible. Overloading users with

technical minutiae can result in confusion, under-
mining the very goal of fostering clarity.

Balancing these considerations demands innovations in
both policy and technology, reconciling the desire for
more open systems with operational realities and commercial incentives.

**Towards a Transparent and Accountable Future: Strate-
gies and Efforts**

To navigate these challenges and cultivate a transparent
and accountable AI ecosystem, several strategies offer
promise:

- **Ethical AI Design**: Integrating ethical considerations throughout the AI design process can
  preemptively address potential transparency
  issues. Design guidelines emphasizing simplicity
  and clarity aid in demystifying AI systems.

- **Third-party Audits and Certifications**: Conducting independent assessments of AI systems can ensure that they meet transparency and accountability standards. These audits can validate claims and
  verify adherence to ethical norms, fostering trust
  among stakeholders.

- **Regulatory Innovations**: Adaptive regulations
  crafted in collaboration with industry players
  and public stakeholders can address the unique
  challenges of AI, providing clear guidelines and
  accountability structures.

- **Collaboration and Dialogue**: Creating platforms
  for interdisciplinary dialogue among technologists, ethicists, policymakers, and the public can
  yield diverse perspectives and drive collective
  efforts towards transparency and accountability.

185

Accountability and transparency are twin pillars that uphold the ethical integrity of AI technologies. As we forge ahead, building systems that are explainable and responsibly managed is essential to unlocking AI's potential for societal benefit. Charting this course requires commitment and collaboration, ensuring AI systems foster equity and trust as they navigate the complexities of a digitally enriched world.

8.5   Ethical Guidelines and Regulation

Imagine navigating a high-speed race car without any guidelines or rules—each driver set loose with their own understanding of the path to the finish line. The result? Chaos, accidents, and a constant sense of peril. The landscape of artificial intelligence (AI) is not dissimilar. Absent a framework of ethical guidelines and regulatory measures, the rapid advancement of AI technologies could lead to societal upheaval, privacy invasions, and unpredictable decision-making landscapes.

Ethical guidelines and regulation serve as the guardrails for AI development and deployment. They provide clarity and direction, safeguarding public interest and ensuring that technological progress aligns with societal values. The establishment of such frameworks, however, is not without its challenges. It requires a delicate balance of fostering innovation while mitigating risks—much like orchestrating a symphony, wherein each element harmonizes with the next to create a coherent and effective whole.

The quest to regulate technological advancement is not a new endeavor. History is rife with examples wherein societies have scrambled to establish rules for emerging technologies and industries. The printing press revolutionized communication, necessitating new laws to address copyright and censorship. The industrial revolution brought forth regulatory measures in response to workplace safety and environmental concerns.

In AI, the urgency for ethical guidelines and regulation is amplified by the technology's capacity to influence and transform various aspects of human life. With AI systems deeply embedded in fields ranging from healthcare to finance, the need for robust regulatory frameworks to safeguard against misuse is paramount.

Ethical guidelines establish principles that anchor AI development in humanistic values. They articulate the moral compass by which AI systems should operate, covering issues such as fairness, accountability, privacy, and transparency. These guidelines are akin to the rules of the road—ensuring all drivers (or AI technologies) can share the space safely and efficiently.

Many organizations and professional bodies have contributed to developing AI ethical guidelines. The OECD's Principles on AI and the European Commission's guidelines on trustworthy AI illustrate global efforts to create coherent, ethical frameworks. These guidelines, while varying in detail, commonly emphasize the need for AI to be inclusive, transparent, and designed for human well-being.

Ethical guidelines provide the groundwork for distinguishing between beneficial AI applications and those that pose risks to society. More than just a moral obligation, they are increasingly seen as a competitive advantage. Companies that act ethically and responsibly are more likely to gain public trust and long-term viability.

While ethical guidelines provide foundational values, regulation translates these into actionable rules and standards. What does effective AI regulation entail? At its core, it must address the pace of AI development, the technology's complexity, and the diverse contexts in which it operates.

- **Pace of Innovation**: In the world of AI, innovation sprints ahead like an untethered cheetah. Regulatory frameworks must be agile, adapting to rapid advancements while providing consistent oversight. Overly rigid rules can stifle innovation; conversely, lax regulations risk enabling harmful practices.

- **Complexity and Unpredictability**: Many AI systems, particularly those using machine learning, consist of myriad interdependent algorithms. Understanding their decision-making is challenging, complicating regulatory tasks. Effective regulation must account for these complexities, promoting transparency and accountability.

- **Sector-Specific Needs**: AI applications vary widely across sectors, necessitating bespoke regulations. For example, AI in healthcare requires stringent safety and efficacy measures, whereas AI in financial markets demands attention to fairness and transparency. Tailored regulatory approaches ensure that each sector's unique challenges are addressed.

One promising model is a layered regulatory approach, combining overarching principles with sector-specific guidelines. This framework ensures that regulations remain both comprehensive and contextually relevant. For instance, overarching laws might dictate data protection and fairness, while sector-specific standards ensure industry compliance.

AI's boundary-blurring nature necessitates international collaboration to develop cohesive regulatory frameworks. Countries worldwide are grappling with how best to regulate AI ethically.

In the European Union, the General Data Protection Regulation (GDPR) has set a global benchmark for data privacy. Its principles not only affect European entities but also compel organizations worldwide to comply, given their global operations.

Similarly, the European Union's AI Act proposes a risk-based model regulating AI technologies based on their potential impact on society. This approach categorizes AI applications from minimal to high risk, applying corresponding regulatory measures.

Elsewhere, countries like Canada and Singapore have championed initiatives emphasizing AI ethics through national strategies and reporting standards. These efforts demonstrate the potential for diverse regulatory frameworks to coexist, adopting unique approaches while aligning with shared ethical goals.

The pathway to effective AI regulation is not solely the domain of governments and policymakers. It requires collaborative efforts between the public and private sectors. Industry leaders, academia, and policymakers must engage in dialogue, pooling expertise to shape viable regulatory solutions.

Public-private partnerships enable the development of industry standards and best practices. The formation of AI ethics boards and interdisciplinary working groups can guide both strategic and operational considerations, ensuring that regulations are informed by practical insights and technological expertise.

Moreover, engaging with civil society organizations and the public fosters transparency and inclusivity. Public consultations provide stakeholders with the opportunity to voice concerns and contribute ideas, engendering trust and broad-based support for regulatory initiatives.

The challenges of AI regulation are manifold, encompassing technical, ethical, and political dimensions. Policymakers must grapple with diverse perspectives, conflicting stakeholder interests, and the continual evolution of technology.

- **Balancing Innovation and Control**: Finding equilibrium between promoting innovation and ensuring responsible oversight is perhaps the most significant challenge. Over-regulation may hinder technological progress, while under-regulation risks societal harm.

- **Addressing Inequality and Access**: Ensuring that all individuals benefit equally from AI advancements requires thoughtful regulatory design. Bridging the digital divide and addressing AI's potential to exacerbate inequalities is essential for ethically sustainable regulation.

- **Alignment with Societal Values**: AI regulation must consistently align with evolving societal values. This fluidity requires adaptable frameworks, capable of integrating new ethical considerations as they arise.

- **Stakeholder Engagement**: Ongoing engagement with diverse stakeholders is crucial for nuanced and effective regulation. Fostering inclusive dialogue ensures that diverse voices contribute to the formulation and evolution of regulatory frameworks.

As AI continues to permeate our everyday existence, establishing robust ethical guidelines and regulations becomes paramount. These frameworks act as the scaffolding upon which trustworthy AI systems are built, ensuring that technological progress enhances, rather than undermines, human dignity and societal well-being. As our AI journey unfolds, let us employ foresight, inclusivity, and collaboration to chart regulatory paths that advance innovation while safeguarding the public good.

Chapter 9

The Future of AI: Possibilities and Predictions

The future of Artificial Intelligence promises to be both transformative and complex, with emerging trends poised to redefine technological landscapes. This chapter explores potential breakthroughs, such as advancements in general AI and increased human-AI collaboration, while assessing their implications for industries and economies. It considers AI's role in addressing global challenges, including environmental sustainability and healthcare innovation. Additionally, the chapter reflects on the broader societal and ethical dimensions of AI's evolution, envisioning a coexistence where AI supports human capacities while posing new regulatory and moral questions.

9.1 AI Trends Shaping the Future

In the not-so-distant past, the realm of Artificial Intelligence (AI) was largely confined to the pages of science fiction and speculative visions of the future. However, as we thrust into the 21st century, AI has firmly estab-

lished itself as a transformative force, redefining industries and influencing countless facets of our daily lives.
The inevitable question thus arises: what trends in AI
will shape our future next?

One of the pivotal trends pushing the boundaries
of AI is edge computing, a movement away from
centralized data processing facilities to the peripheries
of the network where the data is generated.   This
trend reflects a paradoxical shift as technology reverts
to decentralization to solve modern-day problems.
Imagine a world where smart devices, from refrigerators
to city traffic lights, are equipped with the intelligence
to process information locally, reducing latency and
increasing privacy.   Indeed, edge AI promises to
enhance the real-time responsiveness and efficiency of
applications, from autonomous vehicles to advanced
drones, by processing data near the source rather than
co-depending on distant cloud infrastructures.

The potential of edge AI is perhaps best exemplified
in the field of healthcare. Devices like wearables and
diagnostics tools leverage edge AI to provide instant
feedback without the need for external data processing,
thereby safeguarding sensitive health information
and delivering timely patient care. This decentralized
approach ensures that critical decisions are made
almost instantaneously, a feature that could be crucial in
life-and-death scenarios. As we pioneer towards more
personalized and private healthcare, edge AI presents a
crucial stepping stone.

Simultaneously, the evolution of AI is being invigorated
by strides in quantum computing, a field that basks
as much in the light of mystery as of promise. Unlike

classical computers, which process information in binary digits or bits, quantum computers operate using qubits that can exist in multiple states simultaneously. This unique property allows quantum computers to handle a vast number of calculations at unprecedented speeds, a prospect poised to transform AI.

Quantum computing harbors the potential to revolutionize AI algorithms. These potent machines can accelerate the learning curves of AI models, allowing for the rapid processing of enormous datasets. Imagine AI systems in environmental analytics predicting climate patterns with precision previously unattainable, or in pharmaceutical research, where they expedite the discovery of new drugs by simulating molecular interactions more accurately and efficiently than ever before.

While exploring emerging AI trends, the role of sustainable AI cannot be overstated. As society becomes more environmentally conscious, the demand for AI models that are both effective and energy-efficient has intensified. The energy consumption of large-scale AI models, particularly those reliant on deep learning, has raised critical concerns about their ecological footprint. Thus, the future of AI appears inexorably linked with sustainability.

Advancements in energy-efficient algorithms and AI-driven energy management systems represent significant strides in moving towards sustainable AI. For example, Google has deployed AI to optimize the energy usage of its data centers, resulting in a substantial reduction in power consumption. Such progress not only aids environmental efforts but promises substantial cost reductions, creating a dual benefit for enterprises and the planet alike.

The marriage of AI and the Internet of Things (IoT) is
another harbinger of change poised to reshape the landscape of daily existence. As more devices become interconnected, the sheer volume of available data increases
exponentially—data which AI systems can harness for
an array of applications. Consider smart homes, where
AI seamlessly integrates with IoT to create environments
that not only respond to the routines of their occupants
but also anticipate needs, enhancing both convenience
and security.

In industries, this symphony of AI and IoT is laying the
groundwork for what's heralded as the Fourth Industrial
Revolution.   Manufacturing facilities augmented with
AI-driven   IoT   systems   are   transitioning   towards
intelligent   factories   where   predictive   maintenance
and   real-time   monitoring   form   the   bedrock   of
unprecedented productivity.

Additionally, one cannot overlook the trend of AI's
increasing democratization. Innovations in AI are no
longer the exclusive purview of tech titans or research
facilities. Today, more accessible tools and frameworks
allow a broader audience—students, hobbyists, and
small enterprises—to venture into AI development.
This democratization is accelerating innovation, as
varied perspectives contribute to a broader spectrum
of AI applications, enhancing global collaboration and
integration.

With these trends coalescing, AI's role as a cornerstone
of   modern   technology   appears   assured,   but   it
is   not   without   challenges.   Ensuring   that   AI   is

ethical, just, and transparent necessitates vigilance and commitment from all stakeholders involved—developers, policymakers, and the public. As AI's capabilities expand, so too must our approach to its governance, addressing biases and ensuring its alignment with human values.

The transformative potential of AI's future trends paints an exciting yet complex picture. Through edge computing, quantum advancements, sustainable practices, IoT integration, and democratization, AI is moving towards new frontiers that promise to reshape our world in ways both practical and profound. As these trends unfold, they hold the power to define the technological landscape, not only providing solutions to today's challenges but unveiling new horizons as yet unimagined. Development and stewardship of AI must, therefore, balance unfettered innovation with responsible oversight, striving towards a future where AI enriches human life beyond measure.

9.2 Potential Breakthroughs on the Horizon

While the landscape of Artificial Intelligence (AI) bristles with potential, grasping its tangible future developments demands not only keen anticipation but an appreciation for its ongoing journey. The forthcoming breakthroughs in AI are perched at the nexus of fantasy and feasibility, poised to venture into realms of innovation that could revolutionize human existence.

One area intensely anticipated for breakthrough is **general AI**, often shrouded in mystique and popular culture portrayals of thinking machines. Unlike narrow AI, which excels in specific tasks like language translation or playing chess, general AI aims for versatility—machines capable of performing any intellectual task a human can undertake. This ambition harks back to foundational AI endeavors, where scientists envisioned machines that could understand, learn, and adapt indistinguishably from humans.

Historically, the pursuit of general AI mirrors the desire to replicate human cognition. Efforts in the 1950s, bolstered by computing pioneers like Alan Turing, laid the conceptual groundwork, envisioning machines that emulate human reasoning. Although progress has been slow and fraught with challenges, the prevailing hope is that future breakthroughs could unveil systems that grasp context, infer new concepts, and exhibit adaptive learning in dynamic environments.

The breakthrough of general AI would undoubtedly prompt profound shifts across multiple sectors. In **healthcare**, imagine AI systems administering personalized treatment plans, integrating vast spectrums of medical data with a human-like understanding of patient needs. Beyond medicine, such systems could innovate industries like education, crafting individualized learning experiences that adapt to the nuances of human cognition.

Yet, convincing machines to think akin to humans requires breakthroughs in **neuroscience and cognitive psychology**, beyond mere advances in computational power. The ability to decipher and replicate the architecture of the human brain could spearhead the quest for general AI. Thus, progress in these intertwined fields will likely illuminate paths previously concealed in shadow.

In tandem with general AI, the horizon beckons **collaborative AI** as another potent breakthrough. Collaborative AI envisions intelligent agents working alongside humans, enhancing human capabilities rather than replacing them. This symbiotic relationship envisages AI as a partner in problem-solving, decision-making, and creativity.

Picture the business environment, where AI systems analyze complex datasets, suggesting insights that elude human perception. By augmenting judgments with data-driven rationale, such systems hold the potential to transform industries, from finance to marketing, by redefining human roles with AI as a committed ally.

Moreover, collaborative AI portends transformative effects on **creative enterprises**. In music, collaborations between AI and humans have already yielded compositions that juxtapose machine-generated patterns with human artistic vision. This partnership hints at the essence of creative AI: a dynamic interchange where human talent and machine logic coalesce to forge novel artistic expressions.

Equally promising is AI's potential to tackle monumental, global-scale challenges. Consider the breakthrough envisioned in **AI-powered environmental sustainability**. The climate crisis, a formidable opponent of our age, demands sophisticated strategies that AI may provide. From optimizing energy consumption in smart grids to predicting environmental phenomena, AI's analytical prowess could become a crucial asset in curbing environmental degradation.

199

In agriculture, AI-driven solutions are already crafting
efficient, sustainable farming practices. Precision
agriculture employs AI to monitor crop health, manage
resources, and forecast climate impacts, enhancing
productivity while reducing environmental impact.
Future breakthroughs in this sphere could bolster food
security in ways yet to be fully imagined.

The potential of AI to drive breakthroughs in **global
resource management** also deserves mention. With
burgeoning populations and finite resources, optimizing
the allocation and utilization of resources is imperative.
AI systems could lead efficiency drives across sectors
such as water management and waste minimization,
transforming urban planning and ensuring resilient city
infrastructures.

As we gaze into the potential breakthroughs AI
might offer, it's clear that these advancements are not
isolated innovations but interconnected in networked
ecosystems. The interplay between AI and human
ingenuity will shape our collective future, but this path
isn't free from challenges. Ethical considerations, the
integration of these breakthroughs, and navigating
potential disruptions necessitate careful thought and
conscientious action.

As we stand on the precipice of quantum leaps
in AI, the landscape is replete with promise. The
potential breakthroughs in general AI, collaborative
AI, and AI-driven sustainability reflect a world on the
cusp of magnificent change. These trends invite us
all—scientists, policymakers, and global citizens—to
participate in crafting a future where AI's potential is
realized responsibly and innovatively. Though the road

ahead is uncertain, it promises excitement, challenge, and unprecedented opportunity. In embracing this journey, we may yet uncover the profound capacities of AI to enhance, enrich, and perhaps even redefine the essence of human experience.

9.3 Economic Impacts of AI Evolution

As we traverse the rapidly shifting contours of the 21st-century economy, the evolution of Artificial Intelligence (AI) emerges as an influential force capable of redefining economic landscapes. The march of AI from niche technology to mainstream disruptor promises profound implications for productivity, labor markets, and the very structure of industries. In this section, we delve into the multifaceted economic impacts of AI evolution—a narrative woven with potential, promise, and prudent caution.

At its core, AI's contribution to economic productivity is attributed to its ability to perform tasks with enhanced speed and accuracy. Unlike previous waves of technology that automated labor-intensive tasks, AI's prowess lies in its capacity for cognitive augmentation. It not only performs mundane operations but optimizes complex decision-making processes—a change that can sharpen competitiveness across diverse sectors.

Consider AI's role in the finance industry. Trading and investment decisions, once reliant on human intuition, now harness the analytical acumen of AI algorithms that process swathes of data at lightning speed. High-frequency trading systems, powered by AI, analyze market trends with precision, enabling more informed investment decisions and reducing transaction costs. This infusion of AI not only smooths market fluctuations but also creates efficiencies that ripple across the broader economy.

Similarly, the evolution of AI in manufacturing heralds a new industrial era—the "smart factory." Here, AI-powered robots and machines perform precision tasks, predict maintenance needs, and ensure quality control, fostering an environment of unprecedented productivity. The integration of AI into production lines minimizes waste and maximizes output, creating a tangible boost to economic performance.

However, the narrative of AI-driven productivity is not solely about gains. It introduces complexities into labor markets, sparking a discourse laced with anxiety and anticipation. The advent of AI raises perturbing questions: Will AI replace human labor? What will become of workers displaced by machines? These inquiries echo earlier industrial revolutions, where fear of job loss accompanied technological progress. Yet, the nuances of AI differentiation hinge not on displacement alone but positive transformation.

Historically, fears of technology-induced unemployment, such as those voiced during the Luddites' movement against mechanized looms, hinted at labor market horrors that largely never materialized. While certain manual jobs faded, technology paved the way for others—roles that leveraged human creativity and adaptability. In the digital age, AI follows a similar trajectory. While some routine jobs may become automated, AI conjures new labor demands in areas like data science, AI ethics consultancy, and cybersecurity.

The promise of AI for job creation lies in its potential to complement rather than replace human labor. By automating monotonous processes, AI liberates human capabilities for complex, creative, and interpersonal undertakings. Consider the healthcare industry, where AI-assisted diagnostics expedite patient treatment plans, allowing medical professionals more time for patient care. This synergy amplifies human potential, driving economic vitality without sidelining humanity.

Despite these prospects, navigating the transition to an AI-enabled economy requires structured responses to the repercussions on the labor force. Reskilling initiatives, reeducation programs, and adaptable social safety nets become imperative as artificial intelligence impels more dynamic workplaces. Ensuring that the workforce evolves in tandem with technology will be essential to maintaining economic equilibrium.

Beyond the individual level, AI's progression could reshape the structure of entire industries, potentially leading to significant shifts in economic power dynamics. Companies that adeptly integrate AI into their operations may wield competitive advantages, driving consolidation as AI-inept firms struggle to keep pace. This differential capacity to harness AI's power can redefine market leaders in industries such as retail, transportation, and logistics.

The impact of AI also extends to global trade. Enhanced manufacturing capabilities and predictive analytics supported by AI can revolutionize supply chains, reducing inefficiencies and optimizing logistics. For example, AI systems determine optimal shipping routes, forecast demand patterns, and streamline inventory management, culminating in a more agile trade ecosystem.

However, the economic benefits derived from AI might
not disseminate equally across regions and sectors,
potentially intensifying existing inequalities. Advanced
economies with robust technological infrastructures
stand poised to capitalize more readily on AI's
dividends compared to their developing counterparts.
Policymakers must remain vigilant to these disparities,
promoting inclusive growth through international
cooperation, equitable technology access, and the
cultivation of digital skills on a global scale.

Moreover, ethical dimensions of AI utilization orbit
around economic impacts. The concern of algorithmic
biases, where AI could perpetuate societal disparities
or unfair labor practices, looms large. Thus, economic
policies surrounding AI must emphasize ethical
guidelines and unbiased AI deployment to ensure that
technological progress benefits society holistically.

In contemplating AI's far-reaching economic impact, it
is clear that AI promises a fundamental reimagining of
our economic future. Nevertheless, realizing this potential requires measured strategies that balance innovation
with equity, productivity with inclusivity, and advancement with stewardship. The deployment of AI as an
economic powerhouse is not an end in itself, but rather
a means to sculpt societies that thrive in harmony with
their technologies.

As AI continues its trajectory from technology to tradition, it invites us to reconsider and recalibrate notions
of work, value, and economic growth. The impact of
AI evolution is multifarious: it holds the capacity to en-

hance economic productivity, transform labor markets, and reshape industry power structures. Yet, alongside these opportunities, it invites challenges that necessitate thoughtful navigation. Only then can AI indelibly enrich our economic tapestry, ushering in an era where artificial intelligence kindles not just prosperity, but a shared and sustainable economic vision for all.

9.4 AI in Global Challenges

Artificial Intelligence (AI) has emerged not merely as a marvel of modern technology, but as a potential ally in tackling some of the most formidable challenges facing our planet today. From climate change to healthcare crises, AI offers tools, insights, and innovations that could prove pivotal in fostering global resilience. Delving into AI's role in addressing these global challenges invites a reflection upon its capacity to catalyze solutions amid complexity.

Foremost among the world's current trials is the unprecedented challenge of climate change. As the Earth's ecosystems teeter under the strain of anthropogenic activities, the need for robust, sustainable solutions has never been more acute. AI stands as a versatile tool in climate science, offering the ability to model climate systems and predict environmental consequences with precision. Its analytic capabilities enable scientists to process vast amounts of data from satellite imagery, weather patterns, and geological records—data far too complex for traditional computational methods.

Take, for instance, AI-driven climate models that assist in forecasting weather extremes and simulating climate

change scenarios. By incorporating real-time data and
ever-evolving climate parameters, these models help in
understanding potential outcomes and preparing mitigation strategies. Furthermore, AI aids in optimizing
renewable energy resources, such as wind and solar, by
predicting and adjusting to usage patterns and weather
conditions, thereby enhancing efficiency and reliability.

AI's role extends into the gritty foreground of
agricultural sustainability as well. As the global
population surges toward a predicted 9 billion by
mid-century, sustainable food production becomes a
priority of paramount importance. Precision agriculture,
powered by AI, is revolutionizing farming practices. By
utilizing drones, satellite data, and machine learning
algorithms, farmers can monitor crop health, optimize
irrigation and fertilization, and predict yields with
unprecedented accuracy.

An illustrative example comes from the fields of India,
where AI-driven platforms provide farmers with crucial
insights to manage water resources effectively, combat
diseases, and select the best growing conditions. Such
endeavors not only increase productivity but also fortify
the resilience of agriculture against climate-induced ad-
versities.

Beyond the realm of environmental concerns, AI's
potential to transform healthcare and public health
systems is both compelling and imperative, especially
in the face of global health crises like pandemics.
AI algorithms can sift through massive volumes of
epidemiological data, enabling early outbreak detection
and facilitating robust responses. Drawing from lessons
learned during the COVID-19 pandemic, AI-driven

models have been employed to track virus spread, model scenarios, and support vaccine distribution logistics.

In routine healthcare, AI innovation is fostering a new paradigm of personalized medicine. Advanced systems are developing capabilities to interpret genetic profiles, enabling customized treatment plans that align with individual health needs and genetic markers. These systems can predict patient responses to treatments, leading to increased efficacy and reduced adverse effects—an approach that significantly enhances patient care quality.

The utility of AI in addressing global socio-economic disparities further highlights its transformative potential. Access to basic financial services remains a profound barrier to economic prosperity for billions worldwide. Fintech advancements powered by AI are bridging this gap, providing unbanked populations with access to credit, insurance, and banking through innovative mobile solutions. These services employ AI for risk assessment and fraud prevention, broadening financial inclusion in developing regions.

Furthermore, education disparities, often exacerbated by geographical constraints, are also being tackled by AI's reach. AI-powered educational tools can offer personalized learning experiences, adaptively tuning educational content to the learner's pace and style. This adaptability can improve learning outcomes in under-resourced areas, providing a scalable solution to educational inequality.

AI also plays a critical role in humanitarian efforts, where the coordination of logistics and resources can

mean the difference between catastrophe and recovery.
During natural disasters, AI systems analyze satellite
imagery and social media feeds to map impacted areas
accurately and prioritize aid distribution. This rapid
response capability has been seen in action during
deployments in hurricane and earthquake zones, where
AI aids first responders in efficiently allocating scarce
resources.

Another pivotal area where AI can wield significant influence is biodiversity conservation. With species extinc-
tion rates accelerating, conservationists are turning to AI
to monitor wildlife populations and habitats. The use
of AI-powered cameras and sensors in remote locations
helps capture images and audio data, enabling the iden-
tification and tracking of species more efficiently than
traditional methods. This surveillance aids in enforcing
anti-poaching measures and preserving biodiversity.

Nevertheless, as AI ventures into these domains,
it encounters ethical and practical challenges, necessitating thoughtful consideration and oversight.
Concerns include privacy implications of surveillance
technologies, biases inherent in training data, and the
potential for AI solutions to exacerbate rather than
alleviate disparities. Thus, the deployment of AI must
be met with a concerted effort toward developing ethical
guidelines and ensuring equitable access to its benefits.

As we navigate the challenges that define our global
epoch, AI emerges as a beacon of promise and potential.
Its multifaceted applications across climate change,
healthcare, agriculture, and beyond demonstrate
its transformative capability to address key global
issues.   However, realizing AI's potential demands

strategic foresight and moral stewardship to align technical achievements with societal needs. By fostering collaboration between technologists, policymakers, and global communities, AI can truly become a driver of sustainable, inclusive progress, shaping a future where technology enhances the human condition amidst adversity.

9.5 Envisioning a Coexistence with AI

Throughout human history, society has navigated the introduction of groundbreaking technologies that have redefined what it means to work, communicate, and live. With each advancement came an opportunity to harness innovation as a partner rather than a rival. As Artificial Intelligence (AI) continues its inexorable journey from novelty to necessity, we are prompted to envision a future where humans and AI coexist harmoniously— each complementing and enhancing the capabilities of the other. This prospect, both inspiring and daunting, raises critical questions about societal change, ethical implications, and the very essence of humanity itself.

In considering how we may coexist with AI, it is essential to frame the conversation within the broader **historical context of human innovation**. The digital revolution brought computers and the internet into everyday life, reshaping industries and societal norms. Yet, with each wave of technology—from the steam engine to the automobile—initial apprehension gave way to adaptation, leading to an eventual coexistence supported by new social structures and regulatory frameworks.

AI's potential impact is similarly transformative. It

209

weaves into the fabric of our daily lives, serving roles
that range from the mundane, such as digital assistants
scheduling appointments, to the extraordinary, like
autonomous vehicles navigating city streets. In these
trends, we glimpse the nascent stages of a future
partnership between humanity and AI.

An initial step toward envisioning this coexistence
involves redefining the **nature of work and collaboration** with machines. Traditionally, tasks performed by
humans have revolved around routine and repetitive
labor, suitable targets for AI automation. The liberating
promise of AI lies in its potential to relieve humans of
such tasks, allowing us to channel our energies into
creative, strategic, and interpersonal pursuits—areas
where human ingenuity still reigns supreme.

Take the domain of healthcare, where AI augments
human capabilities. Medical practitioners utilize
AI-assisted diagnostics and data analysis to inform
treatment decisions, enhancing precision while retaining
the irreplaceable empathy and judgment that define
patient care. In the workplace, AI-based tools streamline
administrative burdens, facilitating a shift in focus from
process to innovation.

As AI adoption scales, roles in the economy will naturally evolve. Reskilling and lifelong learning become cornerstones of this transition, empowering individuals to
remain agile in adapting to new opportunities and industry demands. Successfully navigating this shift not only
requires personal initiative but also systemic support—
education systems must adapt, and labor policies must
foster both security and flexibility for the workforce.

Envisioning coexistence also demands acute awareness of **ethical considerations** inherent in AI advancement. We must ask how AI systems are trained, to what ends they are put to use, and most importantly, who holds them accountable. History teaches us that with great power comes responsibility, compelling us to prioritize ethical algorithm design, data transparency, and bias mitigation.

Furthermore, this ethical stewardship extends to ensuring equity in AI's benefits. The rise of AI should not widen extant societal divides. Rather, it offers a unique opportunity to bridge gaps when implemented thoughtfully. Access to AI-driven services must be broad and inclusive, ensuring all communities, irrespective of socioeconomic status, benefit from technological progress.

Another dimension of coexistence involves the **cultural and philosophical implications** of living alongside intelligent machines. As AI assumes more roles traditionally occupied by humans, questions arise over how these changes might alter our identity, purpose, and value systems. Voices from the arts, philosophy, and humanities must contribute to these dialogues, shaping AI's integration into a culturally sensitive and meaningful cohabitation.

In creativity, AI has already begun to collaborate with artists to push boundaries of innovation. From AI-generated music to algorithmically devised visual art, these partnerships provoke introspection about authorship and the creative process. Rather than viewing AI as a replacement, it becomes a tool—a new medium through which artists can explore and express unique visions.

211

Societally, embracing AI in education can cultivate
future generations who are not just consumers but
active creators of technology. Educational paradigms
must evolve, promoting digital literacy and encouraging
curiosity-driven exploration of how AI can address
pressing humanitarian and environmental challenges.

Ultimately, envisioning a harmonious coexistence with
AI harkens to a shared future where AI facilitates human
flourishing. The key lies in harnessing AI's capacity to
extend our reach while respecting the intrinsic value of
human characteristics. This vision aligns with a broader
aspiration—leveraging AI not as a detour but as a pathway toward a better world.

The journey to this coexistence is decidedly human, defined by our choices, ethics, and vision. As AI becomes
ever more present, it neither diminishes human worth
nor stands as an autonomous force. Rather, it is a mirror
reflecting our aspirations and anxieties—a partner to be
guided with wisdom and foresight.

As we prepare to share not only our world but our future
with AI, envisioning coexistence becomes a collective endeavor. It is a call to action for thought leaders across
fields and societies, to guide AI's integration with empathy, creativity, and responsibility. Through this synergy,
we craft narratives where technology and humanity advance in unison, forging a legacy of shared success and
enduring value.

Chapter 10

AI and Society: Impacts and Implications

Artificial Intelligence profoundly influences societal structures and daily interactions, prompting an examination of its broader impacts. This chapter delves into how AI reshapes social and cultural norms, affecting employment, education, and public policy. It analyzes the dynamic between AI advances and workforce changes, considering both opportunities and displacement. The chapter also addresses AI's role in governance, emphasizing the need for informed policy-making and regulation. Furthermore, it reflects on public perceptions of AI, recognizing how these views shape its development and integration into societal frameworks.

10.1 AI's Influence on Social Structures

Artificial Intelligence (AI) is not merely a technological advancement; it is a transformative force, reshaping the very fabric of our social structures. To understand the influence of AI on these structures, it is essential to explore how it intersects with various aspects of human interaction—jobs, education, and social connections. This journey illuminates the profound changes AI incites in our daily lives and broader societal dynamics.

Reimagining Employment

One of the most conspicuous impacts of AI is its role in reshaping the job landscape. Until recently, automation was largely confined to repetitive manual tasks. However, AI's ability to learn and adapt has expanded its reach into professions once considered immune. While some fear that AI will lead to mass job displacement, it is equally plausible that it will create new opportunities and demand a re-skilling of the workforce.

Historically, technological evolution has been a catalyst for change, as seen in the Industrial Revolution when machines redefined agricultural practices. Similarly, AI is prompting us to rethink traditional job roles, transitioning from task-oriented work to value-driven intellectual engagement. For instance, in the healthcare sector, AI systems are increasingly used to analyze medical data and assist in diagnostics. They act not as replacements but as collaborators, enhancing the capabilities of human practitioners.

The story of AI and employment is not one of binary outcomes but of nuanced evolution. Instead of mere job reduction, AI can lead to job transformation. For example, the introduction of AI in customer service has automated routine inquiries, allowing human agents to focus on complex issues that require empathy and judgment. This shift highlights a key aspect of AI's influence: it frees cognitive and creative capacities, empowering workers to engage in more fulfilling and rewarding tasks.

Educational Transformation

The ripple effects of AI extend into education, where innovative technologies are reshaping teaching methodologies and learning experiences. Historically, education systems have been slow to evolve, often prioritizing standardized content delivery. AI challenges this paradigm by enabling personalized learning, where students receive tailored material based on their individual needs and learning styles.

In classrooms equipped with AI, teachers transition from content dispensers to facilitators of a more interactive learning process. Adaptive learning platforms can assess a student's strengths and areas for improvement, offering real-time feedback and adjusting the curriculum accordingly. This flexibility not only enhances comprehension but also keeps students engaged by providing challenges that are neither too easy nor overwhelming.

Moreover, AI has the potential to democratize education, making high-quality resources accessible to a broader audience. Virtual tutors powered by AI can bridge geographical and economic divides, offering personalized assistance to learners regardless of their location. Such tools embody the democratizing promise of AI, echoing the potential of past technological advances like the printing press or the internet.

Altered Social Interactions

Beyond the confines of work and education, AI is influencing social interactions subtly yet profoundly. Social media, for instance, relies heavily on AI algorithms to curate content and shape user experiences. These algorithms learn from individual preferences and behaviors, creating highly personalized feeds. While this personalization enhances user engagement, it also raises concerns about echo chambers and the diminishing diversity of perspectives.

AI's influence on social dynamics extends to virtual assistants, like Siri or Alexa, which many users welcome into their lives as companions and helpers. These devices exemplify AI as a benign presence, seamlessly integrated into daily routines. However, their ever-present nature also prompts questions about privacy and the changing nature of human relationships. As we increasingly interact with AI systems, it is crucial to consider how these interactions affect our expectations and understanding of human connection.

In a world mediated by AI, social etiquette is evolving. Consider the virtual meetings that have become commonplace in professional settings. AI-driven tools can analyze meetings to suggest follow-up actions or flag scheduling conflicts, thereby streamlining human collaboration. Yet, this efficiency does not replace the nuanced communication skills inherent to human interaction. Instead, it highlights the need for a balanced coexistence, where AI augments human capability without overshadowing it.

Ethical and Philosophical Quandaries

The pervasive influence of AI invites us to confront ethical and philosophical questions about autonomy, human agency, and the essence of social structures. As AI systems make decisions that affect human lives, we must scrutinize the frameworks guiding these decisions. The issue of algorithmic bias, where AI systems inadvertently perpetuate existing societal prejudices, underscores the importance of ethical considerations in AI development.

Philosophically, AI challenges us to define what it means to be human in an increasingly automated world. The potential for AI to simulate human-like behaviors invites

216

comparisons to historical myths about artificial beings, from the Golem to Mary Shelley's Frankenstein. These narratives illuminate enduring human concerns about technology: its benefits, its risks, and its ability to unearth deep-seated fears and aspirations.

Guardrails in the form of policy and regulation become essential as AI's role expands. These mechanisms should ensure that AI systems are designed with transparency and accountability, safeguarding against misuse while promoting innovation. Efforts to establish such frameworks reflect a long-standing tradition of adapting societal norms to accommodate technological change.

Towards a Collaborative Future

Ultimately, AI's influence on social structures beckons a collaborative reimagining of our collective future. It is not a force to be passively accepted or resisted but one to be actively shaped. By fostering interdisciplinary dialogue among technologists, ethicists, and policymakers, we can ensure that the integration of AI enhances rather than undermines the social fabric.

Case in point, the city of Helsinki has embraced this proactive stance by deploying AI to manage public services efficiently while maintaining transparency about how data is used. This approach not only boosts operational efficiency but also cultivates public trust in AI-driven initiatives.

An equilibrium must be pursued, one where AI is viewed as a partner capable of enhancing human capability and enriching social experiences. By engaging thoughtfully with AI, society can leverage its potential to address global challenges, from healthcare to climate change, fostering a future that is both prosperous and equitable.

In sum, AI's influence on social structures is multifaceted and profound, propelling change across numerous domains. As we navigate these transformations, it is crucial to remain vigilant and adaptable, ensuring that AI's integration into society serves the greater good. This dynamic interplay between technology and humanity continues, driving us towards new horizons marked by possibility and progress.

10.2   Cultural Impacts of AI Development

The development of Artificial Intelligence (AI) is not just a technological triumph; it is a cultural phenomenon that is reshaping the way societies understand themselves and interact with the world. Within this context, AI serves as both a mirror reflecting cultural values and a catalyst sparking cultural change. By examining the cultural impacts of AI, we can gain a richer understanding of how this technology influences belief systems, practices, and norms across different societies.

Reflections of Cultural Values

AI systems are products of the environments in which they are developed, carrying the imprints of the cultural contexts and value systems of their creators. This phenomenon is evident in the language processing capabilities of AI, where linguistic nuances, idioms, and even humor must be culturally calibrated. For instance, an AI that works seamlessly in the United States might struggle in Japan, not only due to language differences but also because of variations in cultural communication styles.

Moreover, the design and deployment of AI technologies often reflect cultural priorities and ethical considerations. In regions where privacy is a paramount concern, such as the European Union, AI development aligns with stringent data protection regulations. Conversely, in countries where technological progress is highly prioritized, AI systems might evolve more aggressively, sometimes at the expense of privacy considerations. These choices signify how deeply cultural values influence AI's trajectory.

Cultural Homogenization and Diversification

The global spread of AI technologies fosters both cultural homogenization and diversification. On one hand, AI's reliance on standardized data encourages a homogenized cultural perspective, sometimes prioritizing dominant cultural narratives while marginalizing others. This can lead to a global culture where Western values, aesthetics, and perspectives become overly prevalent in AI-driven applications like social media algorithms or recommendation systems.

On the other hand, AI also enables cultural diversification by offering tools for preserving and promoting marginalized and indigenous cultures. AI-driven language restoration projects, for instance, work to document and revitalize endangered languages, enabling cultural continuity and empowerment. Similarly, AI is employed in arts and cultural heritage to digitally preserve artifacts and simulate experiences of traditional practices, ensuring that diverse cultural expressions find their place on the global stage.

Shifting Norms and Practices

AI's rise also prompts significant shifts in cultural norms and practices, altering how societies operate on a fundamental level. Consider the tradition-bound world of journalism. AI is now capable of generating news reports and curating content, thereby influencing what is reported and how audiences engage with information. While this automation can streamline journalism, it raises questions about authenticity and the cultural role of human storytelling.

In art, AI challenges conventional notions of creativity and authorship. AI-generated artworks and music compel artists and audiences to reflect on the meaning of creative expression. Does an artwork created by an algorithm possess the same cultural value as one produced by a human? Such questions force a re-evaluation of the artistic process and invite a broader interpretation of what constitutes creativity.

Similarly, in social practices such as dating, AI algorithms play a role in matchmaking, subtly influencing cultural norms around relationships. These algorithms mirror societal biases or ideals but simultaneously challenge traditional relationship practices, creating new paradigms for human interaction that blend technology with cultural tradition.

Cultural Perceptions and Ethical Challenges

AI also invites societies to reevaluate ethical frameworks, prompting discussions around autonomy, agency, and trust. These discussions vary among cultures, as ethical considerations are deeply rooted in cultural philosophies and histories. In societies with a strong emphasis on collective well-being, AI might be embraced as a tool for social good, balancing technological benefits with ethical considerations. In individualistic cultures, the focus might be more on personal rights and freedoms, shaping public debates over AI's role in society.

The ethical conundrum posed by AI extends to issues of accountability and decision-making. As AI systems become more autonomous, determining who is responsible for their actions becomes a complex moral question. Cultural attitudes towards accountability and trust differ, informing how societies reconcile these challenges and adapt their legal and ethical frameworks to accommodate AI.

AI in Cultural Narratives and Mythologies

Fiction and popular culture have long pondered the possibilities of artificial life, from ancient myths to modern science fiction. These narratives set the stage for contemporary dialogues on AI, influencing public imagination and understanding. The portrayal of AI in films and literature—often oscillating between utopian helpers and dystopian threats—profoundly shapes cultural perceptions.

Take, for instance, the myth of the Golem—a creature fashioned from clay and brought to life to serve its creator. This tale encapsulates enduring cultural anxieties about the balance of power between creator and creation, a theme echoed in modern AI narratives. These stories highlight human aspirations and fears around AI, emphasizing themes of control, autonomy, and the consequences of technological ambition.

Towards a Culturally-Inclusive AI Future

Recognizing the cultural impacts of AI encourages a move towards more culturally inclusive AI development. Embracing diverse perspectives in AI design can mitigate biases and foster systems that resonate with a broader range of cultural values. For global technology companies, this means investing in multicultural teams and transcending a one-size-fits-all approach to AI.

Moreover, cross-cultural collaboration in AI policy-making could be pivotal in ensuring that AI serves humanity's shared interests while respecting cultural nuances. Initiatives like UNESCO's ethical guidelines for AI development underscore the importance of international cooperation in creating frameworks that honor cultural diversity.

In essence, AI's cultural impacts are multifaceted, offering both challenges and opportunities. By actively engaging with these dynamics, societies can harness AI to promote cultural enrichment, preserve diversity, and foster global understanding. The nexus of AI and culture, therefore, represents not only a technological frontier but also a profound exploration of what it means to be human in a rapidly evolving world. As we navigate this intersection, the dialogue between culture and AI will undoubtedly continue to evolve, shaping the human narrative in complex and unexpected ways.

10.3 AI and Workforce Dynamics

The dance between technology and labor has always been complex, a tango of advancement and adaptation. With the advent of Artificial Intelligence (AI), this relationship is choreographed into a new, uncharted rhythm. AI stands poised to redefine workforce dynamics across industries, prompting a reevaluation of job functions, skills, and the essence of work itself. Understanding this sweeping change requires exploring AI's role in job creation, displacement, and the transformation of skills within the workforce.

To comprehend AI's impact on workforce dynamics, it bears remembering that history is replete with examples of similar transformative moments. The Industrial Revolution, which introduced mechanized production, serves as a crucial parallel. While initial fears of widespread unemployment loomed, eventually new industries were born, thereby creating jobs that no one had previously imagined. The arrival of AI offers a modern iteration of this narrative, with machines not just replacing human effort but augmenting and transforming it.

One significant aspect of AI is its role as an augmentor, enhancing human capabilities rather than replacing them outright. In sectors like healthcare, AI algorithms assist in diagnosing diseases with remarkable accuracy, enabling doctors to focus on patient care rather than data analysis. In finance, AI streamlines data processing, allowing analysts to devote more time to strategic decision-making. By taking over mundane and repetitive tasks, AI enables humans to concentrate on roles that require creativity and emotional intelligence, capacities that remain distinctly human.

However, AI's impact transcends mere augmentation. It also serves as an innovator, spurring the creation of entirely new industries and jobs. Emerging fields like AI ethics, algorithm auditing, and data stewardship illustrate roles that did not exist a decade ago. Furthermore, the development and maintenance of AI systems create demand across technical and support professions, indicating that AI's adoption can stimulate rather than stifle employment.

Despite the opportunities AI presents, its integration also introduces inevitable disruptions. Certain job categories—particularly those involving routine manual or cognitive tasks—face the threat of obsolescence. Automated systems in manufacturing, logistics, and customer service can perform specific functions more efficiently than their human counterparts. This displacement calls for a proactive re-skilling of the workforce, ensuring that workers transition smoothly into roles where human skills complement AI technology.

The historical pattern of technology displacing and simultaneously creating jobs suggests that workforce adaptation is not only possible but probable. Nevertheless, this transition presents significant challenges. Workers must be equipped with the skills needed to thrive in an AI-enhanced economy. This requires a robust educational and training infrastructure capable of facilitating lifelong learning, adapting curricula to emphasize creativity, critical thinking, and digital literacy.

AI's influence on the workforce extends beyond individual roles to encompass the very structure of work. Traditional hierarchies are giving way to more agile organizational models, responsive to rapid technological changes. AI systems can facilitate decentralized decision-making, providing real-time data and analyses that empower frontline workers. This shift promotes a more collaborative environment, where success hinges on the dynamic interplay between human intuition and machine intelligence.

Moreover, the gig economy—fueled by digital platforms and underpinned by AI technology—illustrates a significant deviation from conventional employment models. Freelancers and contractors rely on AI-driven platforms to connect with opportunities worldwide, breaking down geographical barriers and reshaping the concept of traditional 9-to-5 employment. This evolution highlights a critical reassessment of work-life boundaries, urging societies to redefine what stability and career success look like in an AI-driven landscape.

A closer examination of specific sectors provides further insights into AI's diverse impacts on workforce dynamics. In agriculture, for example, AI-driven machinery and precision farming techniques revolutionize crop management, optimizing yields while significantly altering the roles of traditional farm laborers. Simultaneously, new opportunities emerge in fields such as drone operation and agronomy analytics, blending technology with ecological knowledge.

In manufacturing, AI-enabled robots now assemble products with speed and precision that vastly outpace human labor. Yet this innovation demands skillful oversight, maintenance, and an understanding of advanced production systems, thus shifting job requirements from manual dexterity to technological proficiency. Resilient sectors embrace AI by fostering a skilled workforce adept at managing these new tools.

At the crux of AI-driven workforce change lies the tension between efficiency and humanity. While AI can optimize production and streamline operations, societies must weigh these benefits against the value of human experience and social connection in the workplace. Creating an AI-enhanced workforce that respects human dignity involves addressing concerns about privacy, surveillance, fair compensation, and job satisfaction.

This balancing act requires comprehensive policy-making that supports both technological advancement and worker well-being. Governments and organizations must collaborate to develop protective measures for workers, ensure fair transitions, and uphold ethical standards in AI deployment. Furthermore, fostering inclusive growth necessitates an equitable distribution of AI's economic benefits across different demographics and regions.

AI's impact on workforce dynamics invites us to contemplate the future of work with optimism rather than trepidation. As AI continues to evolve, so must our approaches to education, employment, and economic policy.   By fostering environments that encourage lifelong learning, equipping workers with future-ready skills, and embracing a collaborative mindset, societies can construct a workforce that thrives amidst technological change.

Examples like Singapore's SkillsFuture initiative—an effort to cultivate a culture of continuous learning— demonstrate proactive strategies to equip citizens for an AI-driven world.   Similarly, partnerships between industries and educational institutions can bridge skill gaps, ensuring that training programs align with the demands of a transforming labor market.

The focus, then, shifts from merely preparing for AI's impact to actively shaping it.   By fostering a symbiotic relationship between humans and AI, societies can transcend a zero-sum narrative of jobs lost versus jobs gained. Instead, they can embrace AI as a powerful tool for enhancing human potential, catalyzing both personal and collective progress.

In this unfolding narrative of AI and workforce dynamics, the emphasis on human adaptability and resilience remains key. As the dance continues, it invites us not to resist the rhythm of change but to move with it, choreographing a future where AI's potential is harnessed in concert with human ingenuity and aspiration. This vision of harmonious evolution underscores the essence of an AI-enhanced workforce, grounded in inclusivity, innovation, and a commitment to human progress.

10.4 AI in Public Policy and Governance

In the world of public policy and governance, artificial intelligence holds the potential to revolutionize how governments operate and serve their citizens. By providing tools for data analysis, prediction, and streamlined decision-making, AI can enhance the precision and efficiency of policy implementation. However, with great power comes great responsibility. As AI becomes a fixture in governance, it also raises profound questions about accountability, ethics, and public trust.

AI's ability to process vast amounts of data quickly and accurately makes it an invaluable asset in the policy-making process. From healthcare to transportation, AI can identify patterns and trends that are invisible to human eyes, informing policies that are grounded in robust evidence. For instance, AI analytics can predict disease outbreaks by monitoring healthcare data in real-time, allowing policymakers to deploy resources strategically and prevent epidemics.

Similarly, AI can assist in optimizing urban planning. By analyzing traffic patterns and population growth, AI helps design smarter cities that are better equipped to handle the challenges of urbanization. Such applications underscore AI's potential to transform government operations, making them more data-driven and responsive to the needs of citizens.

AI's introduction to governance is akin to ushering in a new era of streamlined services. Bureaucratic processes notoriously burdened by red tape can be significantly expedited through AI-enhanced automation. Consider the task of processing applications for social services. AI systems can quickly verify eligibility, detect fraudulent claims, and provide real-time feedback, reducing waiting times and enhancing service delivery.

In tax administration, AI can streamline the review of tax filings, flagging inconsistencies for human auditing.   Such automation promotes transparency and fairness, ensuring compliance while reducing errors. Furthermore, AI-powered chatbots can handle a multitude of citizen inquiries, providing round-the-clock assistance and freeing up human resources for complex issues that require nuanced human understanding.

Engaging the public remains a cornerstone of effective governance, and AI has the potential to revolutionize this domain. Sentiment analysis tools can sift through social media data to gauge public opinion, helping policymakers understand citizen concerns and preferences swiftly. This fosters a more participatory form of governance where feedback loops are shorter and policy adjustments can be made dynamically.

Additionally, AI holds promise in crafting personalized citizen experiences.   By tailoring information and services to individual needs, AI can enhance public satisfaction and trust.   For example, AI can help local governments customize community services notifications, ensuring that citizens receive timely information about initiatives relevant to their lives, from recycling programs to public health campaigns.

Despite its potential, AI's integration into public policy and governance is fraught with ethical dilemmas. Ensuring the transparency and fairness of AI systems is paramount. The decisions made by AI algorithms must be explainable and accountable to the public, particularly when they impact lives substantively.

Issues of bias in AI are especially pressing in governance. Historical data used to train AI systems often reflects societal inequities, which, if unaddressed, can perpetuate discriminatory practices. An AI system that inadvertently amplifies bias could result in unjust policy outcomes, eroding public trust. Therefore, it is crucial that governments implement rigorous standards for ethical AI use, including bias mitigation strategies and regular algorithm audits.

Concurrent with ethical challenges are concerns about data privacy. The data required for effective AI applications is often personal and sensitive. Governments must strike a delicate balance between leveraging data for public good and safeguarding individual privacy. Comprehensive data protection frameworks, transparency in data usage, and citizen consent will be essential components of trustworthy AI governance.

Several pioneering examples highlight AI's transformative potential in public policy and governance. In Taiwan, for instance, AI has played a vital role in public health management during the COVID-19 pandemic. By integrating data from multiple sources, AI supported real-time decision-making processes, from quarantine management to resource allocation.

In another illuminating case, Estonia has embraced AI to enhance its digital government services. The country uses AI to streamline the administration of justice, employing algorithms to suggest potential decisions in small claims courts, thereby reducing case backlog. This application allows human judges to focus on cases requiring detailed legal reasoning, showcasing how AI can augment human function without supplanting it.

AI's role in governance is not confined within national

borders; it is a global phenomenon demanding international cooperation. Shared ethical guidelines and standards for AI in governance can foster mutual understanding and collaboration, preventing discrepancies that could lead to conflicts or inequalities. International bodies like the OECD and the United Nations are already crafting frameworks to guide AI use in a manner that is equitable and sustainable across countries.

For effective governance, international regulation of AI is integral to averting challenges like cybersecurity threats and cross-border data flows. Collaborative efforts can ensure that AI technologies are developed with shared human values, while respecting cultural diversity. Such cooperation encourages collective action on global challenges, from climate change to public health, leveraging AI as a tool for common good.

When looking to the future, the potential for AI in public policy and governance is vast, yet certain paths must be navigated with care. Continuous dialogue between technologists, policymakers, and citizens is essential to ensure that AI systems not only serve their intended purpose but do so in a manner that aligns with societal values. As AI evolves, policies must adapt dynamically, fostering an environment where technological advancements complement human oversight.

Education and capacity-building form the bedrock of successful AI governance. Equipping policymakers with the knowledge to understand and manage AI systems will be crucial. Additionally, empowering citizens with the digital literacy to engage with AI responsibly can enhance public dialogue and trust.

Ultimately, the integration of AI into public policy

and governance represents an opportunity to redefine and revitalize how governments serve their people. When harnessed responsibly, AI can help break down existing barriers within government structures, making them more inclusive, efficient, and attuned to the ever-changing needs of society. Through judicious oversight and participatory engagement, AI's role in governance can transcend mere administration, inspiring innovation and reinforcing democracy in the digital age.

10.5 Public Perception and AI

Artificial Intelligence (AI) conjures an array of images in the public imagination, ranging from benevolent aids to omnipotent overlords. How society perceives AI significantly influences its development, adoption, and regulation. Public perception, with its power to shape narrative and policy, acts as both a catalyst for innovation and a brake on technological advancement. Defining these perceptions brings into view a complex interplay between reality and imagination that influences AI's trajectory.

The Lens of Popular Culture

To understand public perception of AI, it is essential to explore its representation in popular culture—where science fiction shapes science fact. Cultural narratives from books and movies create lasting impressions and expectations of AI. Films like "2001: A Space Odyssey" presented HAL 9000 as a sentient, albeit potentially hazardous, AI, solidifying concerns about reliance on intelligent machines. Similarly, "The Terminator" franchise dramatized fears of AI developing self-awareness and aspiring for dominance, coloring AI dialogues with dystopian hues.

Conversely, characters like Data from "Star Trek: The Next Generation" illustrate AI's potential for empathy and personal growth, suggesting that technology can enhance, rather than threaten, human existence. The nuanced portrayal of AI in culture underscores its dual role as helper and harbinger, an ambiguity that fuels public sentiment.

Historical Parallels and Public Sentiment

The public perception of AI bears resemblance to societal reactions to past technological upheavals. During the Industrial Revolution, the advent of mechanized looms spurred the Luddite movement, wherein textile workers destroyed machinery they viewed as a threat to their livelihoods. Similarly, apprehensions about AI displacing jobs persist today—some see intelligent systems as a benefit, others as a bane.

The personal computer revolution provides another historical parallel. Initial skepticism gave way to widespread adoption as society recognized the benefits of digitization. Similarly, as AI integrates into daily life, perception evolves from the unfamiliar to the indispensable, although concerns about job automation and privacy remain.

Trust and Ethics in AI Applications

Public perception of AI profoundly affects trust—an essential ingredient in the adoption of disruptive technologies. Trust hinges on transparent, understandable, and reliable AI systems. Thus, ethics play a pivotal role in technology acceptance. The Snowden revelations brought privacy into sharp focus, prompting heightened scrutiny around data handling and AI's role in surveillance.

Artificial Intelligence applications in sensitive areas,

such as law enforcement and healthcare, intensify ethical concerns. For example, predictive policing, where AI forecasts potential crime hotspots, raises questions about bias and fairness. If AI systems consistently produce inequitable outcomes, public trust erodes. Similarly, in medicine, AI-driven diagnostics and treatment recommendations must be accountable and interpretative, ensuring they align with clinical ethics and human judgment.

Trust is built by demystifying AI, fostering transparency, and ensuring that it complements rather than overrides personal agency. Public understanding grows with initiatives that educate on both AI's potential and its limitations, countering misplaced fears and preventing overreliance.

Regulatory Response and Public Advocacy

Public perception plays a crucial role in shaping regulatory frameworks for AI. Legislators heed citizen concerns, leading to policies that reflect societal values. For instance, the European Union's General Data Protection Regulation (GDPR) reflects public demand for privacy and data responsibility in the digital age. It aims to give citizens greater control over their data while ensuring businesses practice accountability, demonstrating a model for AI governance that puts public trust first.

Public advocacy also influences AI policy. Grassroots movements and advocacy groups call for ethical AI that transcends profit motives to prioritize social responsibility. Initiatives around algorithmic accountability and fairness highlight the demand for systems that remain transparent and equitable, shaping public discourse and policy agendas.

AI in the Public Eye: Practical Examples

Different sectors provide practical examples of how public perception impacts AI deployment. Autonomous vehicles, once the realm of science fiction, have entered reality with trials on public roads. Yet, their development faces barriers reflecting public fears over safety and liability. The infamous Uber self-driving car incident in 2018—which resulted in a pedestrian's death—exemplifies how fears translate into resistance or calls for stringent regulatory intervention.

Conversely, in consumer technology, AI's integration into everyday products has lessened apprehensive attitudes. Digital assistants like Amazon's Alexa and Google Assistant permeate households, becoming familiar aides that highlight AI's practicality over menace. Their widespread acceptance illustrates AI's softening image when perceived as enhancing convenience rather than posing existential risks.

Demographic Influences on Perception

Public perception of AI is not monolithic; it varies across demographics and regions. Younger generations, having grown up with technology, often exhibit less resistance and more excitement toward AI innovations than older counterparts, whose skepticism may arise from concerns over societal change and job security.

Similarly, regional cultural differences play a role. In Asia, particularly in countries like South Korea and Japan, positive perceptions often stem from long-standing cultural narratives that blend coexistence with robots, reinforced by local tech industries. In contrast, Western narratives often pivot around freedom and autonomy, engendering more critical views amid individual liberties concerns.

Efforts to understand these demographic nuances are fundamental for companies and lawmakers aiming to introduce AI responsibly and resonate across diverse cultural tapestries.

Towards an Enlightened Understanding

Ultimately, fostering an enlightened understanding of AI involves decoding the myths, educating the public, and ensuring inclusive dialogues. Public skepticism, while challenging, can drive positive reform, urging developers and policymakers to address biases, enhance transparency, and maintain accountability.

Public initiatives fostering AI literacy, akin to digital literacy campaigns, can empower individuals to distinguish between AI reality and misconception. Engaging with communities through workshops, resources, and dialogues on AI's role and rights can help demystify the technology, alleviating misplaced fears.

As AI continues to grow intricately woven into our societal frameworks, its public perception will play a crucial role in guiding its responsible development and integration. By aligning AI development with societal values and fostering informed perceptions, we embark on a journey towards an AI-enhanced future that cherishes human agency and collective progress. In such a landscape, AI as both tool and collaborator can live up to its potential, serving society in ways that enrich rather than divide.

www.ingramcontent.com/pod-product-compliance
Lightning Source LLC
LaVergne TN
LVHW022340060326
832902LV00022B/4143

9798306036083